Now faith is the substance of things hoped for,
the evidence of things not seen.
Hebrews 11:1

Walking with
FAITH
Stories That Inspire

2016

Copyright © 2016
Mike Rodriguez International
Frisco, Texas

Tribute Publishing

Walking with FAITH
First Edition June 2016

All Worldwide Rights Reserved
ISBN: 978-0-990-6001-3-8

All Rights Reserved. No part of this book may be reproduced, stored in a retrieval system, or transmitted, in any form, or by any means, electronic, mechanical, recorded, photocopied, or otherwise, without the prior written permission of the copyright owner, except by a reviewer who may quote brief passages in a review.

Printed in the United States of America.

In God We Trust

For we live by faith, not by sight.
2 Corinthians 5:7

Contents

Prologue xi

Chapter 1 – Your Navigator 1

Chapter 2 – Life's Defining Moments 5

Chapter 3 – The Heart of Prayer 19

Chapter 4 – Finding Hope Through Love 35

Chapter 5 – Positively Miraculous 49

Chapter 6 – A Second Chance at Love 65

Chapter 7 – Living a Balanced Life 79

Chapter 8 – Goodbye, Mr. Mediocrity 97

Chapter 9 – In the Blink of an Eye 113

Chapter 10 – Bits of Hope 125

Chapter 11 – Dreams, Choices and Paths 143

Epilogue 159

About Mike Rodriguez 161

Prologue

I decided to publish this book because I knew there were others like me who had a story to tell. Others around the world who had faced major challenges they had overcome. Normal people like me and like you that had a story of faith to share or who just needed their voice to be heard.

The contributing Authors in this book, who reside around the world, were brave enough to share their own thoughts, stories, and insights. They did this with the hopes that other people, like you, would find something to take away. Something that would inspire others to make the important changes in their own lives. To understand that what you are going through does not define you, but can certainly refine you to start walking with faith. You can do it, however, you must be willing to believe, to take action, and to start pursuing your greatest purpose to change your life. I would like to tell you that it is going to be easy, but it is not. I would like to say that there is nothing special about the contributors to this book, but that would also not be true. Yet, it would also be false for you to believe that there is nothing special about you, too. You were created with precision, purpose, and your own unique talents. You were also given the ability to know, act on, and use those talents to become great and strong in your own way. Just know, remember, and most importantly believe this, "I can do all things through Christ, who strengthens me." Philippians 4:13 (*NKJV*). As I always say, "Through faith and action, ALL things are possible."

Now let's get you started on walking with FAITH.

> "Faith is more than something you talk about.
> Faith is tested in the moment of battle."
> Mark Turner

Chapter 1

Your Navigator
By Mike Rodriguez

On the day you were born, how wonderful would it be if you were given a map to visualize the purpose for your life? What if you could see the dangers and challenges that you would encounter? What if you could clearly see your path? know that most of us would reroute our maps to avoid obstacles. We would probably select paths that would take us straight to the places that would make us happy. Some of us might even choose a completely different route, taking us somewhere that we think or feel would be better for us. Well here is the reality: that is a "human" life strategy.

Know that your life is not your life. It was given to you, complete with a roadmap, but of course, you do not have the privilege of seeing the roadmap. We must trust in our navigator; the one who holds our roadmap. We do this by having faith.

Years ago I had to meet a client in a part of the Dallas/Fort Worth area that I wasn't familiar with, so I needed assistance to find my way. I typed the address into my navigation system and proceeded to follow the route called out to me

Chapter 1 – Your Navigator

by my device. The journey took me down many familiar roads and places that I had seen before. However, before too long I was driving down a deserted road in an area that I wasn't familiar or comfortable with. I knew something was wrong, but I figured that the navigation knew something that I didn't. I had faith in it and I trusted it.

About halfway down the dirt road, without any civilization in sight, my GPS confidently told me that I had arrived at my destination. I looked around and saw that I was in front of an abandoned gas station. I was frustrated and angry…. and I was lost.

The point here is that we have strong faith in electronic navigation systems that were "built by man," to blindly guide us to our destinations. Yet, when it comes to faith in our almighty navigator, who built man, we might not have the confidence to even get started! This is completely backwards.

We must trust in our creator to guide our path through the divine plan that He has for our life. We must do this with the same confidence and blind faith that we have in our "man-made" electronic devices. This means that you will encounter obstacles and detours, you will have rest stops and delays, and you will encounter extended visits to fun points of interest. You will also end up at places you don't want to be. Through it all you must believe, you must have faith, you must be strong and you must continue to move forward.

Chapter 1 – Your Navigator

If you are saying to yourself, "But wait a minute, I am WAY off course in my life. How can I ever get back on track?" I would say to you don't worry, don't be concerned and don't be afraid. God's plans are perfect.

Just as a good navigation system will correct your path and make adjustments when you get off course; our father will do the same, as long as you are willing to adjust too. Life's situations may seem too big for us, but they aren't for Him.

In my own life, I have followed many wrong paths and made many decisions that took me way off course, while relying only on myself or others. However, I have found that when I follow the truth, He will straighten my path. It is all part of His plan for us to walk with faith as he guides us.

Now go forth and make your life exceptional!

- By Mike Rodriguez

Chapter 1 – Your Navigator

"Life's situations may seem too big for us,
but they aren't for Him."
Mike Rodriguez

Chapter 2

Life's Defining Moments
By Yael Greenberg - Israel

She held me in her arms and her body started shaking. She was overwhelmed by emotions as tears came into her eyes; it was a dream come true for her. She asked him to bring her a chair as she felt her legs failing her. For many years, she had been waiting for this moment – to hold *her* baby in her arms.

I was only nine months old, a small and quiet little baby with clear green eyes. I didn't cry much. Everybody said I was an easy-going baby.

It was Friday morning when they got the phone call they had been waiting on for so long. The person on the phone asked them to come see me at the orphanage. It was a small house with only five babies including me. When they arrived, it was in that moment when my father saw me that he decided they were not going back home without me. Even though nothing was prepared at their home for a baby. They left with their new baby girl!

This is the story of two ordinary people who fell in love and got married. She was 19 and he was 25.

Chapter 2 – Life's Defining Moments

For years, they tried, but could not have a baby. It was only when she was 37 years old that I came into their lives and made them complete! I was born in Israel under a different name. My birth mother, the one I got my genes from, the one that was supposed to take care of me and raise me, never held me in her arms. I spent my first nine months in that orphanage with four other babies just like me. Until the day I got **my first chance in life**. You see, just like in the movie *"Sliding Doors,"* my life could have started totally different if she hadn't let me go. What would my life look like if I had been raised by her? What would it have looked like if I had been adopted by other people?

I was blessed to have an unconditional love from my adoptive parents. From my point of view, they are, and always will be, my only parents. They loved me, pampered me, and gave me all they could, so I could become the person I am today. As a child, while knowing I was adopted, I didn't understand why. Why did she abandon me? Why didn't she want me? Wasn't I good enough for her? How can someone give their child away? I remember reading about how much the first few months of a baby's life, affects the rest of its life. How much impact a touch, a warm and nursing hand, has on a baby's development. I will never know whose hands held me in the first months of my life, but I want to thank them for what they did.

I was a happy child. My parents were hard-working people. My father worked all his life in a factory as a mid-level manager; for almost 40 years he woke up at 5 o'clock every

Chapter 2 – Life's Defining Moments

morning to go to work and returned home at 5 p.m. My mother was working as a saleswoman in a clothing store.

Later on, she started and managed her own store. It wasn't easy for her as well. She opened the shop every day at 8:30 a.m. until 7 p.m. and on top of that, she did all the necessary house chores. It was very important for them to give me the opportunity they never had, so I could get a good education. For many years, as a child and later on as an adolescent, I felt like I wasn't good enough. I felt rejected. It took me years until I could look at my adoption differently, in a positive way. To finally understand that it was a miracle that shaped my life, to see the blessing to be chosen and to have a loving home with unconditional love. You see, after all, my adoption is an adoption and I have decided to look at it differently. Instead of something terrible, I see it as a blessing. This change in my perspective enabled me to release years worth of anger, frustration, low self-esteem, and all sorts of negative feelings.

I studied at the university with an inner duty in mind – to make my parents proud of me. I finished my first degree with honors. I started my career in one of the biggest companies in Israel and made my way from one place to another. My road to success looked promising. At the beginning of the summer of 2002, after I finished my M.B.A., I took a six-month break and traveled to Australia, New Zealand, and Thailand. I was at my peak!

When I arrived in Thailand, I asked my father to join me so we could fulfill our dream to have a vacation together; it was

Chapter 2 – Life's Defining Moments

supposed to be my present for his 70th birthday. He was afraid it would be too difficult and dangerous as he said, "You know… I am not that young anymore." So, he decided to stay home and we celebrated his birthday when I got back. Nine days after that birthday, our lives had changed forever. I will never forget that evening when just a few hours earlier, we were sitting in our small kitchen eating lunch together. Everything was normal until nothing was the same ever again. *My life had changed for the second time.*

It was around 9 p.m. when I got the call from my parents' friends telling me that they were supposed to meet. They told me my mother had called them to let them know they were running late since their car broke down. I tried calling my mother's cellular phone, but there was no answer again and again. I started worrying and kept calling, but still no answer. As a practical woman, after 30 minutes or so, I thought about going to look for them on their way to their friends, but then came the second call. This time from the hospital. I was told there had been a car accident and that my mother was at the hospital. I was asked to come as soon as possible. Do you know that moment when your world is turned upside down, but you don't realize it at first?

On the way to the hospital, I clearly remember thinking, **why** *did the person on the phone talk only about my mother? What about my father?*

I arrived at the hospital, entered the emergency room and asked where my mother was. Someone pointed me to a closed curtain. I pulled back the curtain and saw her. She was

Chapter 2 – Life's Defining Moments

conscious, but couldn't speak. I didn't stay with her too long because I wanted to see where my father was.

The nurses couldn't tell me. They could only tell me that he didn't arrive at this hospital. I asked them to call all the hospitals in the area to find out where he was. Although it was obvious, my mind refused to accept it at the time. I don't remember how much time had passed when two policemen came and asked me if I was Yael. Just like in the movies they showed me his driver's license and asked me if he was my father. Nothing more needed to be said – my world had stopped. Everything stopped. I couldn't breathe. I went inside a small room with a lot of lockers in it. I found myself pounding my head onto these lockers for about 20 minutes: 20 minutes of losing hope, 20 minutes of losing myself, 20 minutes of real grief. After those 20 minutes, something happened to me - I started thinking and realized I had to pull myself together to be able to continue. I had switched on the "autopilot." I needed to take care of my mother.

It wasn't until days later that I found out the details of the accident. My parents were driving on a highway when the engine had suddenly died. The car had stopped in the middle of the highway. My mother stayed in the car and fortunately **didn't take off her seat belt** – this is what saved her life. My father got out of the car in order to put a warning sign on the road. Each car that passed that night had to slow down and bypass them. Except for one. That one didn't slow down. That one crashed right into them. My father was killed on the spot and my mother was severely injured.

Chapter 2 – Life's Defining Moments

The question *"WHY"* came to my mind again. *Why did it happen to them? If they could only have stayed at home as they were supposed to, maybe it wouldn't have happened...*

Having no brothers or sisters, I found myself all alone having to face a series of important decisions like: authorizing the police to conduct an autopsy, deciding what to write on the tombstone and deciding whether to buy a single or a double burial spot. I had never asked them what they wanted me to do in this situation. However, the hardest decision was when and how to tell my mother that my father had died in that accident. That he had taken his last breaths lying on a highway. Since my mother was still in intensive care and was not yet stabilized, I decided not to tell her that my father, her husband, was not with us anymore.

In the morning on the day of the funeral, I was with my mother at the hospital. I couldn't yet tell her because the doctors were afraid she would not be able to bare it and that her medical condition would deteriorate. At the funeral, there were many people; but I was all alone. I was walking beside him as they carried him to the burial spot; tears streaming down my face, I whispered to myself "Daddy where are you? Daddy come back," but he didn't answer. When they all left, I just wanted to lie on the ground next to him and never get up. I couldn't, because I needed to be there for my mother.

The rest of the week I spent at the hospital; in the mornings next to my mother and in the evenings sitting "shiva" at their house. A few days later, she was transferred from intensive

Chapter 2 – Life's Defining Moments

care to a quieter room at the hospital. That was the time to tell her the truth. It was the hardest thing I had ever done in my life.

Over the course of eight months, my mother slowly rehabilitated. During this time while taking care of her, I also had to take care of her store and all the other arrangements that needed to be made due to the accident. This was the busiest time of my life. Slowly, I switched off my "autopilot." Suddenly, I had some time to myself and I felt like a black hole was pulling me in. I felt so much pain, nothing would be the same again. This was too painful for me, all I could think of was *"How can anything be worthwhile anymore? How can I go on with my life without him by my side?"* I asked myself the same question again and again: *"WHY?" Why did it happen to me? Why did it happen to us?"* I had a lot of anger in me.

For months, I couldn't get out of bed. I slept most of the days (and nights), escaping from reality. I didn't want to speak to anyone. I didn't see the point anymore. I remember people telling me that in every "bad" there is something "good." I thought to myself, *"How can there be anything good in the death of a person?"*

They say, "Time heals." Only after time passed by, did I start to see everything that had happened and everything I went through in a different perspective.

One day, I opened the window of my bedroom and saw a bird on a tree. To me, she symbolized life, freedom, and choice. I realized that although I will never be the same Yael

Chapter 2 – Life's Defining Moments

again, the new Yael is one that life has given a chance to see what she is capable of, what she can accomplish. When we direct our lives onto a new pathway, it is a defining moment. That day was the **third defining moment** in my life. That day I asked myself if I wanted to live or die. **Life is stronger than death** - I decided to choose life. That was when something had truly changed in me forever. Just like the first time when I changed *my* perspective, nothing really changed; it was only my decision to look at things from a different perspective that gave me the strength.

Today, I know I have so many blessing from my tragedy – it made me who I am today. It is true that we can't always choose our own path. Sometimes we cannot help it and we are forced into certain situations. But, we can choose how to respond to them. We can choose to accept the situation and be bold, strong, and confident. We can choose to see the good out of *every* situation. Today I know I am strong, bold, courageous, and I am not afraid to deal with what life has to offer me. After all those years, I can proudly say I am what I am. This profound moment had shaped me and my path in life. Anyone who has ever lost someone special knows that from that moment, all the happy moments will be sad as well because of the absence of that person.

My wedding day was a day like that. I remember the moment before walking down the aisle, the music started playing and it was then that I felt his absence, like a big hole in my heart. My heart ached because he could not hold my hand and be there with me and give me away. Although he was absent in body, I felt he was there in my heart. I know that he was

Chapter 2 – Life's Defining Moments

proud of me and especially for the one I've chosen to be my husband.

I've seen people and heard stories about people who have had their own share of personal battles. I've learned that each and every one of us has their own special strength inside. We don't always see it, but when the time comes it suddenly pops out and takes control - it helps us to overcome.

I know that I have much more to go through in life – I am ready. I will always do my best, try hard, develop and learn, be a better person, and never give up! My experience taught me that even at difficult times, when things aren't going the way I planned, when it seems every way I turn I get a ***NO***, I can still find ways to reach my goals and fulfill my dreams and I'm not going to give up any one of them! I choose to strive for the best in everything I do, to be faithful to my heart, true to myself, and to always remember to accept only a ***YES!***

I truly believe that *you*, yes ***YOU*** reading these lines, are strong and ready for life! Wherever this story catches you, know in your heart that you have it all within you. Remember it is *your* life, *your* choices, *your* game, *your* voice.

I wish that you will look at this moment in your life with a smile coming from your heart. Remind yourself you can choose how to look at what happens to you. Choose to look at it in a positive way and you'll see that you will feel great.

Chapter 2 – Life's Defining Moments

These are my ten principles for life:

1. Life is stronger than death.
2. Defining moments happen – it's up to us to decide how to respond to them.
3. In difficult situations don't ask "Why?" ask "How can I benefit from it?"
4. You are stronger than you think you are - Trust yourself!
5. There is always a way – find the Yeses in your life! They will show you the way.
6. It is not *what* happens that matters, but *how* we choose to look at it that matters – find the positive!
7. Choose love. Choose to accept, learn, and grow from what life brings to your door.
8. In the end, we are left with our memories. Make sure these memories count.
9. Thank God for all you have here! Today! Now!
10. Never forget to use the seat belt in the car!

- Yael Greenberg

Chapter 2 – Life's Defining Moments

About the Author – Yael Greenberg

Yael is a passionate and energetic speaker, business consultant, wife and mother. She is happily married to Yair and they have two wonderful boys.

Yael was born and raised in Israel. You could say her passion to help others started with her military service. At the age of 18, she joined the Israeli Defense Forces and helped soldiers to overcome financial and personal problems. She began her studies right after that and graduated with a B.A. in Economy and Logistics with honors. In 2002 she finished her M.B.A. specializing in HR.

Chapter 2 – Life's Defining Moments

Yael got her corporate business knowledge while working for the largest companies in Israel. Finally, in 2007 she sought to pursue her dream of helping business owners maximize their personal potential in order to improve their business. This dream materialized very quickly. During the last nine years, Yael has accumulated vast knowledge in marketing, logistics, operation, accountancy, finance, management, human resources and more, due to the large diversity of her clients.

Today Yael is a Ziglar Legacy Certified Speaker, a certified business consultant by the ministry of economy and immigration of Israel. Due to her experience accumulated during the last 17 years, combined with her personal skills, she brings Ziglar's powerful messages in her own special voice that touch people's hearts and motivate them to action. "My mission is to awaken people to realize their full potential, to be the driving force for action and to help you make groundbreaking changes quickly and for good!"

Yael would love to hear how this story affected you.

Yael Moskovitz Greenberg
Phone: 972-52-8466455
Site: www.I-Deliverit.com
E-Mail: Yael@I-Deliverit.com
LinkedIn: www.linkedin.com/in/yaelgreenberg

Chapter 2 – Life's Defining Moments

"It is true that we can't always choose our own path. Sometimes we cannot help it and we are forced into certain situations. But, we can choose how to respond to them."
- Yael Greenberg

Chapter 3 – The Heart of Prayer

Chapter 3

The Heart of Prayer
By Mark Turner - Texas

I have taught Bible Class for over 30 years now. In that time, on numerous occasions, I have instructed brothers and sisters on the power of prayer. The most recent lessons were part of a series entitled, "The Circle Maker." In this series, participants are encouraged to circle their requests to God. This can be done by simply writing them down and going over them with confident bold prayers daily.

I have been running laps at the local high school track and would, in my mind, put those people and the things I desperately wanted to pray about, in the middle of the football field and I dedicate a prayer the entire lap for each one. I understood the power of prayer from an intellectual standpoint perfectly. Like most of you, I believe in prayer. Like most of you, I understand the need for prayer. Like most of you, I comprehend the mechanics of prayer. Unlike most of you, or perhaps not, I have had those times in my life where I wondered, *Is this working? Does this really help? Is God hearing my pleas?*

Chapter 3 – The Heart of Prayer

Little did I know that I would not only discover the importance of prayer, but I would experience firsthand the awesome power.

Mark 11:24 says, "Therefore I tell you, whatever you ask for in prayer, believe that you have received it, and it will be yours." NIV

My wife Cathy and I live in the town of Wills Point, Texas located directly between Dallas and Tyler. We headed out early in the day on Thursday, April 11, 2013, to Monroe, Louisiana to attend an "Evening with the Robertson's" event hosted by the Duck Dynasty family. What a great evening and fun time. We headed back home the next day, taking our time and doing some shopping in Shreveport before getting home in the early evening on Friday night.

I woke up Saturday morning about 7 a.m. and didn't feel quite right. Suffering from a sleep disorder, I use a CPAP machine to help me breathe at night. I removed the mask and simply felt like I could not get a really deep breath in. I got out of bed and went into the bathroom and tried to wake up a bit more by doing some knee bends and stretching. I couldn't shake the feeling and was still unable to take a true deep breath. You know the kind of breath I'm talking about where you breathe in and your entire chest fills with air and when you let it out you get a relaxed calm. I continued to stretch, thinking that perhaps I had pulled a muscle and after 10 minutes or so returned to bed thinking that I would just relax and begin to feel better.

Chapter 3 – The Heart of Prayer

As I lie in bed, I began to run through some relaxation steps. I would breathe through my nose and out my mouth slowly in an attempt to rid myself of this strange sensation. I don't know how long for sure that I remained in bed, but after a period of time, I decided that I needed to get up and move and see if I could get over this. I'm stubborn for certain. I returned to the bathroom and was doing my best to take deep breaths and stretching my arms high in the air. I must have been making quite a bit of noise and it caused Cathy to yell out, "What's all the racket in there? You sure are making some strange noises." About the time she asked that question, I felt a sharp pain shoot down my left arm. I yelled back, "I think I'm having a heart attack." With that, Cathy jumped out of bed and called 911. She then ran to the bathroom and immediately gave me four aspirins. I had sat down by this point and was doing my best to try and relax.

Our daughter Katie was home from college and Cathy had roused her out of bed. I made my way to the living room and I could hear the siren of the ambulance in the distance. While we live inside the city limits, most GPS systems show a road to our house that does not exist. I could hear the ambulance heading in the wrong direction and told Cathy to call them back and instruct them on how to get here. As my breathing grew even more shallow, I got on my knees and bent over the couch, held my arms against my chest and remained there as I once again heard the ambulance miss our road exit. I told Katie to get the car out of the garage because she would have to take me to the top of the road as I didn't think I would live until they got to me.

Chapter 3 – The Heart of Prayer

While she was in the process of getting the car, the ambulance finally arrived. While I didn't believe I was going to live, I was never in a panic state and remained calm. I didn't think about it much at the time, but looking back now, I understand that faith is more than something you talk about. Faith is tested in the moment of battle and without thinking about it, my faith kept me calm.

Mark 9:23, "If you can?" said Jesus. "Everything is possible for one who believes." NIV

I had enough strength that I met the paramedics at the door and climbed on the gurney myself. They took my vitals, said my blood pressure was OK and they connected me to the E.K.G. The E.K.G. reading was not normal, but was not showing anything to be alarmed about. I told them that something was really wrong so they gave me a nitroglycerin pill under my tongue and loaded me up for transport.

Wills Point is about 55 miles away from Baylor Hospital. To make the trip longer, the ambulance driver took the most out-of-the-way path. Since the nitro tablet had brought no relief, the paramedic was instructed en route to give me another one. Like the first one, I felt nothing. Two nitro tablets and it was if I had taken two more aspirin. My dad used to say that it felt like the top of his head would come off when they gave him one, yet here I was having taken two with no effect on me whatsoever. Cathy and Katie were following the ambulance and calling friends to start a prayer chain for me as headed toward the hospital.

Chapter 3 – The Heart of Prayer

"...The prayer of a righteous person is powerful and effective." James 5:16 NIV

Arriving at Baylor, I was hustled into the emergency room where nurses and the emergency room doctor immediately surrounded me and started taking an assessment of my condition. The doctor read the E.K.G. and said it looked fine. When I replied that the paramedic said the same thing, I again stated something was wrong. Her reply was, "That's not the only indication. We see people die with a good E.K.G." (So much for bedside manner.) She explained that they perform a series of tests, E.K.G. being one, to determine what is going on. Another is a blood test.

I don't remember the exact test, but I remember the doctor saying they would take blood right now, check the enzyme they were looking for and then check me again in two hours. I was feeling OK by now and was ready to go home, but was now stuck in a two-hour window. The initial test came back as a .7. The doctor said in healthy people it is .3-.5 so she said something could have gone on, but they needed to wait for the next test. The enzyme had something to do with heart muscle damage. Two hours later the number was 1.7. It had more than doubled and indicated that something had happened and they needed to figure out what. They admitted me to the heart hospital for further tests, observation and a heart catheterization.

After being admitted around 1 p.m. on Saturday, the barrage of tests began.

Chapter 3 – The Heart of Prayer

I knew something was wrong when a nurse gasped at my most recent blood test levels about four hours after I had arrived. The enzyme had jumped to a 10. It would later top out at 33, which was off the charts. A heart surgeon later told me that they don't usually speak to people with levels of 10 or greater, as they are usually in the morgue. Comforting, right?

I still felt OK and was sitting and talking like nothing had happened. I was simply awaiting my heart catheterization which was scheduled for Monday morning. After a sleepless Saturday night, due to incessant caretaking, blood draws, blood pressure, temperature, toe and finger counting, etc., I was dog-tired on Sunday morning.

About mid-morning, I mentioned to Cathy that my left arm was hurting a bit. I thought I might have laid on it wrong or perhaps it was the bed. I know, what a dummy. She and Katie both told the next nurse that entered the room. Like magic, there were six people that appeared out of thin air surrounding my bed. Blood was immediately drawn, pressures taken and people were moving very quickly. The heart doctor walked in, didn't say a word, pulled the paper from the E.K.G., barely looked at it and said, "Get him to the catheterization lab right now."

How quickly life changes, I thought to myself. I have heard this phrase and said this phrase a thousand times. At that moment, for truly the first time in my life, I understood it.

Chapter 3 – The Heart of Prayer

As the team was prepping to move me, one of the nurses asked, "Are you nervous Mr. Turner?" I answered, "Not at all." I had an unexplained peace about me. I kissed Cathy and Katie goodbye and flew down the hall to the surgical room.

Philippians 4:7, "And the peace of God, which surpasses all understanding, will guard your hearts and your minds in Christ Jesus." ESV

Once again, I moved myself to the table and it looked like a starting gun went off somewhere; everyone was in rapid motion. The speed and precision were something I had not witnessed before and a surgical nurse told me not to worry as they only operate at that pace within that room. They practice and work at that speed regardless of the patient status.

Right before they started the procedure, the doctor told me I could watch on the large monitor just above me to my left. The monitor looked like a 60 inch TV and would assist in guiding the catheterization through my arteries. I told him I would sit this viewing out. I felt the wave of twilight hit me and the odd sensation of being able to hear what was happening, but somehow I did not care or feel anything. It was an odd contradiction in senses. At one point in the procedure, the doctor asked someone if the pain in my chest had been in the front or the back. I recall answering him, "The front doc."

Chapter 3 – The Heart of Prayer

When the procedure started, I could feel a lot of wetness running between my legs. My thought was, *Hey that's my blood*, but somehow it was no big deal. I don't really know how long the procedure took, but when it was finished the doctor patted me on my left ankle and said, "We're all done, Mark." I responded, "What did you find?" He said, "We can tell where an event occurred as we see the damaged area, but your arteries are in great shape and they are probably cleaner than mine. It looks like your body cleared itself (remember these words). You are a lucky man."

I was taken to recovery where a man stood over me for two hours holding pressure on the insert point for the catheterization in my leg. When they tested my blood in the recovery room, it had thickened to proper levels in the short trip down the hall. They said it takes most people an hour or two and while they didn't have an explanation why mine was so quick, they were all happy nonetheless.

At the end of two hours, pressure was removed, no bleeding was evident and I was wheeled back to my room. About an hour later a nurse came in and asked me if I thought I could walk. As a way of an answer, I swung my legs over the bed, stood up and said, "Let's go."

While resting later that day, I received a phone call from one of my best friends in the world, Rick. Cathy had called him on the way to the hospital the day before to tell him what was going on.

Chapter 3 – The Heart of Prayer

Rick asked me if I was ready for my catheterization procedure on Monday. I informed him that the schedule was moved up and I had it today. He was eager to hear the outcome, so I explained what the doctor had said. Rick became silent to the point I thought we might have lost connection. "Are you there Rick?" I asked. "Yes Mark, I'm still here, but you are not going to believe what I'm about to tell you brother." "What is it?" I asked. Rick explained that he was at home the day before, when Cathy called, as she followed the ambulance to the hospital. After Cathy filled him in, he went to find his wife Jan. Jan was in their bathroom drying her hair. Rick filled her in with all the details and they decided to stop everything right then and go into their bedroom to pray. Rick said they got down on their knees at the side of the bed and started to pray over me and my heart. Jan is a fervent prayer warrior and Rick said she pleaded with God to "Please let Mark's body clear itself." The exact words the doctor used.

It was as if the air was sucked out of the room. The impact made me speechless and my eyes filled with tears. I have prayed thousands of prayers, but can honestly say that I had never understood the true impact of prayer until it happened to me.

That very day, while I was in surgery, my home congregation was gathered and praying as well. When they had said, "Amen" one of the member's phone rang and they were given the news. God's timing is awesome.

Chapter 3 – The Heart of Prayer

The power of prayer impacted more than me that day. I don't know why God chose to show His favor on me in that way that very day, but I am eternally grateful He did.

That Sunday night, my phone rang and I looked down and saw it was from Texas Dermatology Associates, my dermatologist office. As you can imagine, I was thinking, *Why would they have these automated calls on a Sunday night?* I had been to a regular checkup appointment the prior Monday and they had discovered a spot on the bottom of my left foot in the middle of my instep. They had taken a biopsy (ouch, ouch, ouch) on Monday and it would take several days for the results to come back.

I answered the phone and the young man told me he was with the office and was calling as my test results were back. How strange I thought, a follow-up call late on a Sunday evening. He said, "Mr. Turner, your results are back from your biopsy and you have Stage 2 melanoma." I began to laugh and he said, "Mr. Turner, this is serious, why are you laughing? I told him I was in the heart hospital and now he calls to inform me that I have melanoma, so he should go to my house and shoot my dog because bad things come in threes. We laughed and then he said we would have to excise as much of the area as possible and we should do it as soon as possible. I told him I would call them when I got released from the heart hospital.

Back-to-back issues caused me to start feeling a bit like Job.

Chapter 3 – The Heart of Prayer

When the head of the heart division visited my room on Monday morning he said, "I just had to come and meet the guy who came in here, had such high levels, and is going to be released today with no balloon procedure, no stent, or no open heart surgery. We can't explain what happened, but we know the outcome." I looked at him and said, "I can sure explain it. The power of prayer."

On the way home from the hospital, I mentioned to Cathy that if I was going to have to take it easy for a few weeks, I wish we could go ahead and get the melanoma surgery done as soon as possible. We walked into our house and the phone rang and it was the dermatology office telling me they had a surgery cancellation for Tuesday and was wondering if I wanted it. God was listening for certain. The surgeon found out I was just released from the heart hospital and decided it was too risky for anesthesia so they would have to do the entire surgery, including skin grafts, with local anesthetic. Ouch, Ouch, Ouch. I wouldn't wish that on anyone.

God was once again watching over me and they were able to get all of it and after months of recovery, I was able to walk again.

Knowing prayer is great. Understanding prayer is even better. Gathering wisdom from prayer is the greatest. Experiencing prayer is life-changing. It's my prayer for each of you reading this to not wait until tragedy hits to become more sensitive to God's answers to your everyday prayers.

Chapter 3 – The Heart of Prayer

When you begin to realize that they are continuously answered, you will notice that your prayers get bolder. We serve an awesome God. Nothing is too big for Him. Pray bold and audacious prayers. Who knows, you may even get the sun to stand still.

- Mark Turner

Chapter 3 – The Heart of Prayer

About the Author – Mark Turner

Mark Turner is a lifelong resident of Wills Point, Texas. He has been married to Cathy for over 36 years and they have two wonderful children, Grant and Katie.

Mark has spent his entire career in the communication's sector in technical and leadership positions. He has lived abroad and traveled extensively during his career.

Most recently, Mark was the President and Chief Operating Officer of Value-Added Communications (VAC). VAC was sold to its largest competitor several years ago and Mark continued as a consultant for a three-year period until deciding to become a full-time speaker and trainer. Mark is the founder of a motivational, business building and personal improvement company named N2Success.

Mark has taught Bible Class for over 30 years and preaches many times a year at his home church. He is a Ziglar Certified Speaker and Trainer and a Certified Human Behavior Consultant with Personality Insights Institute. Inspiring leadership and propelling relationships to greatness are passionate areas Mark covers in his keynote addresses and training. Mark loves to provide training using the D.I.S.C. Model of Human Behavior. He says, "Where else can people have so much fun, learn so much insight into themselves and improve every relationship they have all in one session?"

Mark can be reached at mark@n2success.com.

Chapter 3 – The Heart of Prayer

"Knowing prayer is great. Understanding prayer is even better. Gathering wisdom from prayer is the greatest. Experiencing prayer is life-changing."
Mark Turner

Chapter 3 – The Heart of Prayer

Chapter 4

Finding Hope Through Love
By Pieter Van Der Westhuizen - South Africa

I was born in 1981 during the apartheid era in South Africa, and I saw first-hand the effects that it had on our country. When I was 13 years old, apartheid ended and South Africa turned into what was considered to be a free and democratic country. I can also tell you that things did not change the way we expected to. Anyone that lived in South Africa during the apartheid age and still lives here now can tell you that things are not necessarily better or worse. Let me explain.

Jim Rohn famously said that "For things to change, you have to change." This is a very true statement, but change is not easy if people are not willing to walk in love and work together. Immediately after apartheid ended, a lot of the old, experienced, white individuals left their positions of work because of their unwillingness to change. At the same time, many new black employees and managers did not want to take advice from the existing white people in their positions. They did this out or fear or maybe even arrogance. This was not good news for our country and we can see that clearly today.

Chapter 4 – Finding Hope Through Love

People can only do what they know. If someone does not know how to do something, then it is silly to have expectations that they will be able to do it properly. Also, for people to be able to do things effectively, they need to be willing to humble themselves and be willing to learn. This can only be done if people treat each other with the respect and love that only God can give. Today we see the effects of our country's infrastructure falling apart due to mismanagement of funds, corruption, and a lack of knowledge. This is happening because the old generation did not want to pass down their experience and the new generation did not want to take the old generation's advice.

In South Africa today there are still a lot of things that are not right, but I can also say that there has been a lot of change that was really good for the country. New, young leaders are rising up to make a difference, but it would have been a lot easier if we were just willing to work together to build this country into a wonderful nation. This can serve as a wonderful lesson to us all, knowing if we would only be willing to learn from each other through love and respect, the world can be a better place.

As I got older, I realized that if I wanted to live a full and happy life, I needed to create my own path devoid of other people's opinions. I believe that so many times in life we form an opinion of someone not based purely on our own experience and interaction with them, but based on opinions that were imposed on us by others. This is a recipe for disaster. The people that influence us may not necessarily be the best people for us to be around.

Chapter 4 – Finding Hope Through Love

I believe that every person is influenced by the people around them. As a child, it is very hard to change that fact. As an adult, you have a choice. Even though I was incredibly shy as a child and young adult, I knew that I wanted to make a difference in the world. I just didn't know how. I had a lot of friends and more or less an idea of what I wanted out of life, but I wasn't really sure of how I was going to achieve it. Looking back now, I realize how naïve and unprepared I was for my future.

Even as I started my working career as a young adult I always knew that there was something more I needed to do with my life. I always did my best when I started working at a new company and loved learning new things. I usually started getting bored when the job was not challenging me anymore. I now realize that it was because God had much bigger plans for me than I had for myself.

Remember that God is a loving God, and no matter what happens in your life, God has a way of letting everything turn out for your best interest. Well, for me it was definitely like that. No matter how many times I changed my career, or how many times I made silly rash decisions, God always had my back. I can now see how He guided me into becoming the man I am today.

I always had a good relationship with God, but I think my breakthrough in my relationship with Him came when I was in the Military in 2003. The Military can be a very challenging and emotional place to be. It can, however, also be a very rewarding place and that is where my relationship with God was truly strengthened.

Chapter 4 – Finding Hope Through Love

The years following my military service had many ups and downs, but my biggest challenge came in September 2009. I was 27 years old, and my wife and I were on our way to a spring dance in the neighbouring town where most of my family lived.

On our way to the dance, we were hit head-on by a driver who completely disregarded the traffic laws by overtaking another vehicle where he shouldn't have. I never saw him coming as there was another vehicle in front of us that swerved just before impact. There were so many miracles happening at that point, and because of that, I can be here to share my story with you. First, when my wife tried to phone the ambulance call centre, no one picked up the phone. She then proceeded to call my sister, who was waiting for us at the spring dance. Even though she was inside the dance hall with all the music, she managed to hear her phone.

My sister happened to know a paramedic and he just happened to be on duty at that moment. Not only that but they were already on the same road we were on, having tended to a less serious accident. They were on their way back to the hospital, so they turned around and headed out to us. Due to the massive impact, I had internal bleeding and I was literally drowning in my own blood, and when the paramedics arrived I was just barely breathing. If they were to have come directly from the hospital, then they would have been too late.

Waking up in the hospital the next day, I found out that I had a crushed right elbow, a shattered left kneecap, damaged

Chapter 4 – Finding Hope Through Love

liver, kidneys, and lungs. I had torn several muscles in my right leg and my chest was ripped to shreds. I did not have even one scratch on my face. I can truly say that God is always present and protecting you, and no matter how bad it may seem to you, He always has a plan. These days, when I reflect on my life, I constantly remind myself of Job 1 verse 12, where God told satan that he may touch everything Job owned, but that he may not take his life. I have seen many times throughout my life how satan tried to destroy me, but God had bigger plans for me. No matter what happened, God always made something good out of it. Now don't get me wrong, I didn't always see the good, but looking back now, I can. Remember that we only see a small part of the picture, but God sees the whole canvas. We just need to trust Him.

Now, I started this chapter speaking about love and respect and the willingness to learn from each other, and I would like to elaborate a little. People can sometimes say the silliest stuff not taking into account what they are actually saying. To put this into perspective I have to tell you about the person that caused my accident. According to eyewitness accounts, he disregarded all traffic laws and overtook where he was not supposed to. He was also driving while under the influence of alcohol. Unfortunately, he paid for his mistake and recklessness with his life.

After the accident, people would ask me what happened to the other driver. When they heard that he had passed, many would say that it was good. That hurt me deeply because my wife and I were the ones hurt in the accident, and we didn't feel any sort of madness or hatred towards that person. It may sound extremely harsh, but how many of you have said something similar when you heard of something bad happening to someone you know, or even to yourself. Saying things like that is not walking in love. Remember that I am not saying that I never felt that way throughout my life, but as I strengthened my journey with God I realized that I needed to walk in love no matter what, just like Jesus did. While the people were crucifying Him, beating Him and calling Him all sorts of names, In Luke 23 verse 34, *[34]Jesus said, "Father, forgive them, for they do not know what they are doing."* (NIV)

We tend to judge people from our own perspective. We forget that other people may have something happening in their lives that may be causing them to act in a certain way. If we walk in love, we understand that other people are doing things according to what they know. We need to love them regardless of what they did, where they come from, the colour of their skin, or the language they speak. We as people can only learn from each other if we walk in Godly love.

Just think about it. You will never take advice from someone that you despise or don't trust, but if someone you respect, gives you advice, you will gladly take it. We as human beings are just infatuated about proving that someone else is wrong and that we are right. We should understand that God wants us to walk in love and peace. Remember that your actions and not your words should show who and what you are.

Chapter 4 – Finding Hope Through Love

When you walk in Godly love, your example will lead people to open their heart to what God can do in their lives. I believe that the biggest damage we can do to the Kingdom of God is to be hypocrites. Let your words and your actions be aligned and show that you are a child of God walking in Godly love.

In the world today, it is considered okay to wear what you want and say what you want because it is a form of expression. We as humans have the right to express ourselves. However, if I go to somebody on the street and tell them that what they are wearing is offensive to me and they should take it off, they would be truly offended because I am not allowing them an opportunity to express themselves. However, people find it okay to force somebody to remove a cross or a religious symbol because it offends them. This is not walking in love. We need to respect people for who they are and what they believe in. We need to love them and pray for them and let God work in their hearts. If we walk around judging people, then we are not walking in Godly love. When we are judging people, we are causing them to close their hearts to hear what we, and ultimately God, wants to say to them.

When things get tough, we are left with a choice. Are we going to sulk about it, or are we going to rise above it? After my accident, I was declared medically unfit to do the job that I was trained for. I was 28 years old and was told that for the rest of my life I would not be able to earn a living in my trade. Initially, this was a devastating blow to me. However, as I stated earlier, God will let everything work out for your

Chapter 4 – Finding Hope Through Love

best interest. Within less than 10 months I had a better job with the same company paying a better salary. One thing I have to mention is that your results are directly related to your attitude. I have a saying that "Your bounce-back is directly proportional to your attitude when you're at the bottom." This means that when you sit and sulk and you are just a rotten person to be around, you cannot legitimately expect to receive abundant breakthrough. Use your diversity as a message. When you walk with Faith, believing that God will take care of you and all your needs, then you can be happy no matter where you are.

Before my car accident, I used to be an incredibly shy person. To give you an idea, I used to say that I would never do sales or public speaking. However, God has bigger plans for us than what we have for ourselves. In a little over five years after my car accident, I now own two businesses: one in South Africa and one in the USA. I was the first Ziglar Certified speaker in Africa and I absolutely love working with people. I realize now that it was not that I didn't want to do sales or public speaking, but that I was afraid of it. Fear can often hold us back from doing the wonderful things that God has planned for us. We need to be willing to do things afraid. Fear can be a very powerful tool and it can keep you safe in times of danger. That is the way God made us, but we should never let fear stop us from pursuing something that God placed in front of us to do.

A while back I got involved in ministry and through the process, I believe that God showed me some things. As I mentioned earlier in the chapter, I spent a large part of my

Chapter 4 – Finding Hope Through Love

life unsatisfied and believing I was meant for bigger things. What I realized is that we as humans will never find the true peace we are looking for. Now before you get upset, let me explain. The reason I say this is because I believe that we (humans) are not from here. What I mean by this is that we are spiritual beings in a physical body placed on this planet to serve God. While I was spending some time with one of my pastor friends, I jokingly said one day that we are spiritual beings in a physical body sent on a mission by God, but we have amnesia. We can't remember our mission, and we have to figure it out. When we figure out our mission and complete it, we get to go home to our Father who sent us. This can many times be very frustrating, but walking in Godly love is the crux of all our missions.

We as Christians know that we are here to serve God and we need to bring people to Him. We can only do that through love. No one ever changed or became better because someone judged them. They become better because someone loved them the way they were. Through example, they showed them how to *do* and *be* better, but they were led to make the choice themselves. We need to do our part and let God do the rest. I also believe that if we make ourselves available, then God will use us. Don't think that God can't use you where you are right now. Often, just a single act of kindness can make a huge difference in another person's life and through random acts of kindness, we can change the world. Also, remember that your children will not do what you say, but they will do what you do, so show them how to be a kind, loving person that treats everyone with respect.

Chapter 4 – Finding Hope Through Love

Finally, to end, I want to say that we need to walk in Godly love every moment of every day. We need to show through our actions that we are children of God. We need to treat all people with the same amount of respect regardless of who they are, where they come from, what they do, or how much they earn. Remember that God died for all of humankind on the cross, even though most of the world rejected Him. Even today most of the world rejects His love, and that is why we need to show the world the love of God, that no matter what we did or how we acted in the past, the love of God and blood of Jesus is eternal.

Remember that in Mark 12:30-31 Jesus said this: *"^{30}Love the Lord your God with all your heart and with all your soul and with all your mind and with all your strength. ^{31}The second is this: 'Love your neighbour as yourself.' There is no commandment greater than these."* (NIV) And in Matthew 22:40 it says that *"On these two commandments hang all the Law and the Prophets."* (KJV)

I believe what Jesus is saying here is that if we truly walk in Godly love, with true love for each other, then all of the other commandments will also fall in place. This will happen because there is no way that we will do any evil towards the ones we love with God's love. God's love completes all things, and that is why He sent Jesus to die for us, so we can learn to walk in the same kind of love as Jesus did.

Please go into the world and show them the love of God. This is the way to peace and happiness and most importantly, to eternal life in the presence of God the Father, Jesus Christ the Messiah, and the Holy Ghost.

Chapter 4 – Finding Hope Through Love

May God bless you abundantly in your journey and may you experience His love every second of the day for the rest of your life.

- Pieter Van Der Westhuizen

About the Author – Pieter Van Der Westhuizen

Pieter Van Der Westhuizen was born as the youngest of five children in a small mining village near Witbank on the Highveld of Mpumalanga, South Africa.

Pieter grew up as a very shy boy and because of his shyness, he always felt like he struggled to fit in. Pieter, however, loved the outdoors and spent most of his spare time in the

Chapter 4 – Finding Hope Through Love

forest surrounding the village. He spent many years teaching himself how to overcome his shyness. This led to many achievements throughout his life. By the age of 34, Pieter had worked as a Boilermaker Artisan for more than 12 years, as a project buyer and he has spent time in the military as command post assistant and radar operator in both the South African Army and Air Force. Pieter also holds a private pilot's license and is a licensed financial advisor.

After a devastating head-on car accident in September 2009, Pieter had to radically re-shape his life. Since then, he has become the first Ziglar Legacy Certified Trainer in Africa and has been involved with motivational speaking and coaching since 2012. Pieter has an incredible insight into what makes people function at their peak and he is very passionate about making a difference in the world, while helping others to achieve more. Pieter believes that with God all things are possible and he lives his life that way.

You can contact Pieter on the following platforms:
E-mail:
pieterwest@live.co.za   or   pieter@breakingthezone.com
Linked-In: za.linkedin.com/in/pieterwest
Website: www.breakingthezone.com
Facebook: www.facebook.com/PieterWest.Motivator

Chapter 4 – Finding Hope Through Love

"When you walk with Faith,
believing that God will take care of you and all your needs,
then you can be happy no matter where you are."
- Pieter Van Der Westhuizen

Chapter 4 – Finding Hope Through Love

Chapter 5

Positively Miraculous
By Ken Warren – North Carolina

Miracles happen every day and most everyone has a miracle happen at some time in their life. Often we dismiss these supernatural events as coincidence or luck and soon forget about them. I encourage you to recognize them, appreciate them, and learn their deeper meaning.

Your miracle may be a life-changing event and have a profound effect on your future. I had such an experience in 1990.

In early June that year, my father had a stroke. A bad one. He was in the local hospital battling some digestive issues when it happened. There was some question as to how it occurred as he was scheduled to be discharged that morning, but they found him on the floor by his bed with his subclavian tube pulled out. My brother called to give me the news and described his condition as unresponsive. "Get here as quick as you can," he said.

Unresponsive...that word kept playing over and over in my mind as I rushed home from the West Coast trade show I was working. It is human nature for us to be concerned

Chapter 5 – Positively Miraculous

about the unknown, and *unresponsive* was surely a big question mark for me. I tried to stay positive and prayed for healing. I thought about all the great times we had enjoyed with Dad and about how a poor outcome would affect our family. Thoughts of what was wrong and what could have happened kept flooding my mind. I tried desperately to shake off any bad thoughts. I knew I needed to put forth a brave face for Mom, my wife and my toddler son.

After a torturous journey and a quick stop home to tell my wife what was happening, I hurried to the regional hospital where they had transferred Dad for more intensive care. As I entered the hallway toward his room, I saw a longtime friend and neighbor in the hallway crying. My heart sank as I thought I was too late. Luckily my brother stepped out of Dad's room into the hall and from the look on his face, I instantly knew Dad was still with us. Seeing Dad lying there, I became painfully aware of the gravity of the situation and just how "unresponsive" he was.

The next few days were long and tedious. Mom, my brother and I spent a lot of time in the hospital. We talked to doctors, nurses, relatives and friends, but there was no real change in Dad's condition. Every few hours a doctor would show up and do some tests. They would scratch Dad's foot and get no response. They would sometimes use a mild shock to his feet and still nothing. They would also shine a light in each eye checking to see if his pupils would constrict and move it around to see if he would follow it. Again, no acknowledgment.

Chapter 5 – Positively Miraculous

Dad was breathing on his own and his vitals were OK, but there were big questions about damage to his brain. The doctors were very careful in choosing their words, but it was obvious they were preparing us for a very bad prognosis. Some of the nurses, while very kind and caring, were a little more open about the severity of his stroke. Their expectations were not positive at all.

On the fourth day, the lead doctor on Dad's team told us that while the recovery from a stroke is unpredictable, this case was not looking good. Getting no response from stimuli this far from the event was a very bad sign. Although Dad was not moving around, he had started to curl up. I thought it was due to some stroke damage, but a nurse told me that he was beginning to assume a fetal position which again, was not a good sign.

I decided to spend the night at the hospital again and encouraged my brother and Mom to go to their respective homes and try to get some much-needed rest. I settled in the recliner next to Dad's bed and prepared for a long night. The doctors and nurses were coming less frequently and the "testing" was mostly forgotten now. I tried to sleep, but I was not very successful. What I did do that night, was talk to God, a lot. I will admit I did not simply ask for recovery, I pleaded. I asked in every way I could for his healing on my terms. I even tried to formulate a deal God would find acceptable. Some promise I could make in trade for Dad getting better, foolish of course, but I was desperate.

Sometime well after midnight, I accepted that God's will is supreme. I acknowledged that I did not understand his plan,

Chapter 5 – Positively Miraculous

but knew that he had a purpose and it was for the best. I knew we needed a miracle and I asked for exactly that. Just as a child asks a parent for what they want openly and with no shame, I asked for that miracle. I begged for it.

I reached across the bed rail and took hold of Dad's hand. It felt good to hold it, even though when I squeezed his, he did not squeeze back. I held his hand and talked to him. It was all I could do.

As dawn approached, a Bible verse popped into my head…"I will lift up mine eyes unto the hills, from whence cometh my help." Psalm 121:1 KJV.

We were in the hospital in Asheville, NC, surrounded by the beautiful Blue Ridge Mountains. I focused on the mountain top directly out the hospital room window where the very beginnings of the coming day showed its gentle outline. Daybreak was upon us as I once again asked for God's help. This time, I prayed for his will to be done and if possible, for that to include healing for Dad. At that very moment, the first rays of sunshine broke over the mountain and seemed to reach directly to Dad. He ever so slightly squeezed my hand.

I nearly jumped out of the chair! *Did I really feel that? Did I want to, so badly that I imagined it?* I squeezed his hand again and it was not as limp as before. I moved my hand slightly and Dad wiggled a little closer to me. Hallelujah! I moved a little more and so did he. I knew prayers were being answered and that I was witnessing a miracle. The wave of emotion that flooded over me is indescribable.

Chapter 5 – Positively Miraculous

Now you can think I am being overly dramatic and that this seems like a scene from a made-for-TV movie, or that I have a vivid imagination. I don't care. I was a witness to what transpired and I know who orchestrated every single detail.

Over the next hour, Dad moved a little more and even made a few faint sounds. When the nurse came in to check on him, I told her things were getting better and he was beginning to respond. His reaction to her examination was not impressive, so she was understandably skeptical. I was undaunted in my excitement. Another hour or so passed and my brother came back for the day. I could hardly contain my joy as he too saw the improvements. Dad was now beginning to blink his eyes and his slight grunts told us he was coming around. We stopped a passing nurse and asked her to confirm the reactions and tell the doctors what was happening. She could see the changes as well and promised to relay this to his care team.

Soon one of Dad's doctors came in to examine him. By now, Dad was making more noise and moving around a little more. When he tried the flashlight, this time, Dad recoiled a little. The doctor looked up at us and smiled. He knew something spectacular was happening.

As the day passed, many doctors and nurses came by to check on Dad. There was a new energy in the room and they all felt it and wanted more. The prognosis was upgraded, although it was expressed with guarded optimism. We were warned that we had entered uncharted territory. Dad was so much better than they could have even hoped for at this

Chapter 5 – Positively Miraculous

point, and they had no comparison to use as a guide to where he might progress.

Over the next few days, Dad steadily improved in what even the doctors described as "miraculous fashion." He was communicating with us and recognized close family and friends. It was clear however, he was often confused by some things that should have been familiar and he was very weak on his left side. I questioned the doctors on the next steps for his recovery. It was explained that Dad would need much rehabilitation and that if we chose that, it could be on an out-patient basis.

Then the doctor addressed his mental state and his memory. He said that a stroke as severe as Dad's, created significant damage to part of his brain. The memories and functions that were contained in those damaged sections were gone. He went on to say that the damage also broke many of the connections or synapses that guided information across one part of the brain to another. The good news is that the brain can modify synapses to create alternate pathways and even build new ones to bypass the damaged sections. This re-routing and new construction take time, but there should be continued improvements in Dad's condition. He warned us that the modified signal routing would never be as efficient as the original, but it would certainly be better than nothing.

The best thing we could do was be patient and supportive. A lot of how well Dad would do was up to him and in keeping a positive attitude. We took him home and signed up for rehab.

Chapter 5 – Positively Miraculous

It did take time, but Dad's memory certainly came back. He was able to make huge gains in his strength and stamina.

While his employer forced him into medical retirement, Dad returned to teaching his Sunday school class and even built a house. He formed a musical group and provided entertainment for church gatherings, fundraisers and numerous assisted living facilities as a part of "his ministry." The same assisted living centers where we once thought Dad would need to move to, were now dependent on him for regular recreation for their residents.

I have no doubt that Dad's recovery is due to his indomitable spirit, God's grace and in no small part to a positive mental attitude. We have all heard about the power of positive thinking and the doctors acknowledged it was an important part of his recovery. If a positive mental attitude is so powerful and important, there must be more we all should learn.

Knowing the miracle of Dad's recovery was meant to have a broader reach, I began to search for what underlying message we were meant to receive. I am convinced it was to share the power of positivity, so I tried to learn all I could about staying positive even in adversity. To help the most people, we need to look at how both faith and science agree on this powerful force.

There are countless examples of how positive thought has helped people overcome seemingly insurmountable obstacles. Dr. Norman Vincent Peale, Zig Ziglar and many more have long shared stories of these triumphs and

Chapter 5 – Positively Miraculous

encouraged us to focus on the positives. If you have not enjoyed the works of either of these great leaders, I urge you to do so. But, how does science support these beliefs?

Let's revisit what the doctor said about rebuilding synapses. I am no scientist, so this explanation is in very simple layman's terms. Throughout the brain is a collection of synapses which are structures that permit a nerve cell to pass an electrical or chemical signal to another. In between each of these synapses is some empty space known as the synaptic cleft. When you have a thought, one synapse fires a chemical across the cleft to another synapse building a temporary bridge upon which the electrical signal can cross. This signal carries along with it the information you are thinking about.

Even more amazing is that every time this electrical signal crosses the cleft, the synapses draw closer together, decreasing the distance the electrical signal must cross. It is a very, very minuscule change, but repeated after time, it can make a measurable difference in the signal's travel time. The brain is constantly building and rebuilding these bridges for thoughts to cross. Every thought follows this same formula, but not the same path. Remember the thoughts you have most often, shorten the distance between the synapses and decrease the time it takes to form the bridge and deliver the thought to your consciousness. The brain is essentially rewiring itself, changing its circuitry to compel the same synapse path, to fire together making it easier for the thought to process.

So what about negative thinking? The brain processes pessimistic thoughts by exactly the same procedure it does

Chapter 5 – Positively Miraculous

positive thoughts. These thought impulses travel at the same speed, but as you would expect the shortest distance usually wins the race. So that means if you consistently think positive thoughts you have shortened the travel time for optimism and it will most often overtake the negative thought.

This means that thought truly does reshape your brain. It is possible to change the way you process information and in essence, change the way you think. You can train your brain!

If you want to be a great golfer, it takes training and many hours of practice to become proficient. Same thing for a basketball player, tennis player, musician, artist, speaker and a host of other activities. In Malcolm Gladwell's book *Outliers*, he puts forth the idea that to become a master at anything, it takes approximately ten thousand hours of deliberate practice. It is a good read and gives many examples from various walks of life to make the point. Whether it is an athlete's muscle memory, or a researcher's experimentation or a laborer simply getting the job done, after that number of hours you have likely mastered the skill. So how long does it take to put in ten thousand hours? For most people it is about ten years.

Now, don't let negativity creep in. It may take a number of years to become a master, but you can begin to be more positive today! Many articles report that you can form a new habit in as little as twenty-one days. Several psychologists say it is not that cut and dried, but that you really can begin to see "automatic results" in about sixty-six days on average. Whether it is twenty-one days, sixty-six days, or even a little more, those days will pass regardless if you choose to be

Chapter 5 – Positively Miraculous

more positive or not. If you decide to reap the benefits of the awesome power of positive thinking, you will see the results in a short amount of time and with continued practice, become a master.

So starting right now, every time you have the opportunity for a reactive thought, choose positive over negative. It is that simple. I did not say it is easy, but it is simple. When an event happens, good or bad, you can choose to be thankful for the experience and explore the lesson to be learned. Dad's stroke was certainly not a good experience, but accepting that it occurred, rejoicing in his recovery and finding the lesson attached has generated a positive result. We must be realistic and understand sometimes the negative synapse path will temporarily prevail, but know there is nothing to be gained from negativity and move to a positive thought as quickly as possible.

So, if this has not caused your head to explode yet, get ready. It is not just your thoughts that can rewire and alter the synapse pathways, but the thoughts of those around you can do it too. When you see someone else experiencing an intense emotion, be it anger, frustration, joy, etc., your brain tries to employ the same synapses to help you understand the emotions you are observing. We typically refer to this as empathy. This is how we share sadness during a tragedy, or develop a mob from a group of normally calm individuals. I am sure you have seen an agitated person calm down in the presence of other peaceful people.

Motivational speaker, Jim Rohn said, "We are the average of the five people we spend the most time with." I think our

Chapter 5 – Positively Miraculous

brain trying to emulate the synaptic path of those we associate with explains why this is true. Both inside and outside, thoughts affect you so be careful who you share your time with and how you let emotions flow. Negative people will certainly cause you to be more negative. That does not mean you should avoid friends who are going through a rough spot, they need your support. However, choose to spend most of your time with people who are positive and uplifting, if you too desire to live a positive life.

If you met my father today, you would never guess he almost left us twenty-five years ago. He has overcome more medical maladies than anyone else I know and spent more time in hospitals both before and after the stroke than any person should. Every morning he wakes up smiling and happy to be with the people he loves, one more day. I try to follow his example.

Nowhere, have I found that practicing negative thinking produces a positive result. There are no stories of how negativity overcomes adversity. A group of negative thinking people do not generate a solution to a problem. Sometimes you must acknowledge dissatisfaction or a problem, but let that lead to a positive path to the solution.

So what will you choose? The world is unpredictable. You will get your share of joys and sorrows, of incredible highs and crushing lows. You may experience situations that would devastate some people, and other times be on top of the world. How you handle these events will depend on your faith, how you have trained your brain and who you associate with most often.

Chapter 5 – Positively Miraculous

I urge you to be as positive as possible and when you experience a miracle, look for the lesson that comes along with it.

Enjoy your blessings,

- Ken Warren

Chapter 5 – Positively Miraculous

About the Author – Ken Warren

Ken began selling with his first job in a men's clothing retailer at the age of fourteen and continued into college. At nineteen he bought a retail shoe store and that year he was introduced to Zig Ziglar at a business conference.

Zig's message resonated with Ken and his course was set for a career in sales. After leaving retail, Ken worked as a territory manager and then national sales manager for several top companies in the hearth and barbecue industry.

Chapter 5 – Positively Miraculous

In 2000, he opened a sales and marketing agency to more correctly focus on helping clients reach their goals. In 2007, Warren Marketing Group was recognized by Entrepreneur Magazine as one of the Top 500 fastest growing privately held companies in America.

Ken has led North American sales for distributors and top manufacturers including Coleman, KitchenAid and Swiss Grills. That business continues to thrive and the team has won numerous awards for sales and service. Ken believes success comes with a responsibility to give back to the community. He serves in multiple positions on industry boards and committees, as well as helping sponsor several charity barbecue events supporting education.

In 2014, he seized the opportunity to study with the Ziglar organization and become certified to help carry the legacy and teachings of Zig Ziglar, who inspired him years ago.

Ken is happy to utilize his forty plus years of sales, marketing and management experience to help you reach your goals.

You can contact him at:

Warren Marketing Group
888-297-0238
Ken@kenwarren.coach

Chapter 5 – Positively Miraculous

"You may experience situations that would devastate some people, and other times be on top of the world. How you handle these events will depend on your faith."
- Ken Warren

Chapter 5 – Positively Miraculous

Chapter 6

A Second Chance at Love
By Arthur Brite - Ohio

As a pastor who came to faith in 1992, I continue to pray daily for strength and guidance knowing that spiritual war exists 24/7. The minute you let your spiritual guard down, your faith can be compromised. No one is immune and yet, we often get "comfortable" in our walk. It's then that we let the secular world desires and challenges, as well as the dark forces of evil, take front and center in our actions and plans. Does this make us weak Christians? No, it means we are His people who must trust in His plan, knowing it is through His grace that we are saved. The operative phrase is "His Plan" which is often clouded by our everyday challenges.

No one is immune, no matter how long you have been saved or how strong you believe your walk is daily. If it sounds like I am talking from personal experience, then I am GUILTY AS CHARGED! How can I possibly show any cracks in my armor, when I preach to others and willingly give spiritual guidance? Well, I do. I internalize my challenges and weaknesses at times, rather than giving them to my Savior.

Don't be anxious about anything, but in everything by prayer and petition with thanksgiving, present your requests to God.   Phil 4:6 (NIV)

Chapter 6 – A Second Chance at Love

Since I have been a Christian for the past 24 years, would I consider myself safe from any more of this spiritual warfare? The answer is no. I faced a very emotional and spiritual challenge in 2012 when my marriage was ending. How could I have let this happen? I did most (okay, let's be honest, it's more like some) of the right Christian things and felt my faith was strong, but spiritual warfare? Would I walk the walk I had preached to so many others? I wish I could tell you yes, but truthfully, I was weak. My first move was to turn to My Father for strength and guidance, but as the divorce process lingered on, I did it less.

My kids were very concerned as they saw me fall deeper into depression about where my life was headed and what the future looked like. My finances would be decimated and I would now be alone.

How did I not see this?
How did I let my family down, emotionally and financially, as the spiritual leader?
Where was the hope I told others He provided, through His Grace?
Did I no longer trust My Father? Was my faith really this weak?

I was an emotional mess filled with anger, fear, confusion, frustration, sadness, embarrassment, failure and so much more. Where was the emotional stability I spoke about in my motivational presentations? I refused to confide in or open up to others. I was embarrassed and angry that I had failed so many, including myself and My Lord. My kids approached me about counseling and held me accountable to get help.

Chapter 6 – A Second Chance at Love

I believe that Our Father will never give us more than we can handle. We are to turn to Him for His Grace in taking on spiritual as well as secular challenges.

I can do all things through Him who gives me Strength. Philippians 4:13 (NIV)

I found myself at my absolute lowest and I felt little hope. I just needed to turn to My Father who was there for me the whole time. I would like to tell you that I rose up out of the ashes and had one of those climactic epiphanies that you see in movies. (You know the ones where the hero gets this wide-eyed look as an amazing revelation becomes apparent and the story changes.) It looks great on the screen, but it is not exactly reality. There are Bibles in my office, bedroom, and briefcase, so the signs were never far away. So what made me turn to my faith, when it had not been my major focus, as I wallowed deeper into despair?

Hollywood would have lightning bolts, fire, and inspiring music playing as I rose out of the ashes. The reality is that I felt lost as I sat at my desk looking at the Bible. I felt it was untouchable since I felt I was now unworthy. Yes, this is how fragile we can become in spiritual warfare. I wouldn't even talk to my Christian friends or siblings, even as they begged to talk with me about what was happening. So what made me open the Greatest Book ever written? Him! He knew I was at my lowest and so vulnerable. It was time for Him to bring me home to where he would be able to save me for His Plan. I read some and prayed some, but I still felt lost and hurt. When would this ever turn around? Oh yeah, just ask for his help and guidance.

Chapter 6 – A Second Chance at Love

Through His grace, He will save you! Just like those V8 commercials where they slap themselves in the forehead, I wondered, *How have I let my faith become so clouded?* We all do, so don't beat yourself up or believe you are always safe from evil.

The road back was neither short nor immediate because I still felt weak, but daily I came back to The Word and prayed. I told my two sons that I was done with relationships. I was alone, but not lonely! Yes, I was still living my plan, not His. I had done such a stellar job with my plan, why would I not follow that path? People encouraged me to get help and socialize. Would I eventually look to move into a relationship? No. I had a plan to be alone the rest of my life, but apparently this was not His plan! Thank you, Lord, because what transpired next was truly one of those profound moments in my life. I told others I would not do online dating or really put much of an effort into that area of my life. Well, being alone turned to loneliness. He does not want us to be solitary creatures, but rather serve others through His Grace.

I remember this moment every day because of the profound impact it had on my life, my family, and my faith. There I was, feeling lonely when I turned to My Father in prayer.
"Father, if it is Your plan for me to be alone the rest of my life, then I will accept it. However, if you could possibly put a strong Christian woman in my life, I would be so grateful."

BAM! It happened for me.

Chapter 6 – A Second Chance at Love

The Lord knocked me over by putting the name, Beth Williams, in my heart and mind. Beth Williams? My first girlfriend from 9th grade and yes, my first love! I hadn't spoken to her in years and only a few times in the last 43 years.

This wasn't just a tap on the shoulder or a wink; it was that V8 hit to the forehead with a warm hug! I felt that if God had put this in my heart and mind with such a powerful and immediate message, then I should certainly check it out. So, where would I start Lord? I had not kept in close contact with my classmates, but had just been to a reunion the year before. I had to ask my daughter, Lindsay, how to request a friend on Facebook to see if she was even in the area, let alone available or interested. My daughter laughed as she rolled her eyes and showed me how. I finally located Beth, but her profile picture was clearly from another country. Oh well, that takes care of that option. What the heck, I decided to give it a shot anyway.

God had made such a profound and powerful gesture that I had to at least try something. I got a response back that she had accepted me as a friend. Okay, so now what? I had been out of the dating game for so many years and felt I wasn't very good at it anyway. I saw she was single, so I asked where she lived in the world. Fortunately, she was only 10 minutes away! The picture was from her medical mission in Peru. Are you kidding me? Would she like to go to lunch to talk? Yes!

We both were guarded because of past relationship failures and trust issues.

Chapter 6 – A Second Chance at Love

She had come to faith in the 80s and would become such an amazing, profound, and loving impact on my faith, my family, and my life. As we talked that day, we carefully played our cards on what had happened in the many years since we had seen each other. I had an amazing time and couldn't stop thinking about her. She told me the same thing and we began to see each other regularly. My kids wanted to know who this woman was who had dad so smitten. I needed dating tips about dinner plans from my daughter, about where I should take Beth. This was truly the Christian woman who was changing my life and it was awesome.

My depression, anger, fears, frustrations, and definitely loneliness were subsiding. Yes, He does have a plan for each of us, just ASK HIM in prayer.

Don't be anxious about anything, but in everything by prayer and petition with thanksgiving, present your requests to God.   Philippians 4:6 (NIV)

Commit your actions to the Lord, and your plans will succeed.   Proverbs 16:3 (NLT)

My friends and family saw the change and were so happy for me. My son, Kyle, came home to visit and walked in the door to meet Beth. She put out her hand to shake his and he said, "Anyone who makes my dad this happy gets a hug!" A huge bear hug followed and I knew he approved. My son Jonathan gave the same response and now all three kids saw what I had seen: an amazing, loving, Christian woman who was changing their dad's life and our family.

Chapter 6 – A Second Chance at Love

I felt so blessed to have Beth in my life, but how would I make sure this relationship would grow strongly and faithfully? Once again, I was starting to make it my plan, not His. I met her two daughters and three grandchildren. When you are young, it is all about getting the parent's approval on your relationship. When you are my age, it is about getting the kids' approval. The Lord has blessed me with wonderful relationships with all five. Beth and I attended her church where I was introduced to many Christians who had battled with life's challenges. Through faith, they were saved and redeemed. Their testimonies were as heart-warming and joyous as mine. Beth was opening my faith to the world of Christians that I had previously closed out. Forty-three years had changed our lives, but not our hearts. We loved each other! We knew this was part of God's plan to be together for each other and our families. Prayer and faith had brought my first love back to help me walk our path of faith together.

I could not imagine my world without her. I wanted to make each day permanent for so many reasons. However, even though our love was strong, trust had been compromised in each of our lives, previously. Was this truly where we should go together and was this best for everyone involved? The easy answer was yes, but we needed to learn more about each other over the next few months. Were there bumps in the road and differences of opinions? Yes, just like any other relationship. We were brutally honest with each other on faith, politics, families, friends and even music. We were too old to play games and hide our feelings. If this was going to work, we had to trust in His Grace that He had a purpose of reuniting us in love and faith.

Chapter 6 – A Second Chance at Love

We had begun dating in December of 2013 and quickly knew we wanted to be together every day. Remember, I was the guy who told my sons I was never getting serious, let alone married again. If they saw any signs of this, they were to do whatever was necessary to bring me back to reality. *Uh boys, are you taking notice of what is going on here?* Trust me, they absolutely were taking notice and laughed about my words. There was no stopping His plan.

I proposed on April 4, 2014. Beth and I were married on October 4, 2014, in front of family and friends.

It was a beautiful day of love and faith where two people committed before God, to fulfill His plan. The ceremony was officiated by the pastor, who I collaborated with on the vows, since I had also conducted wedding services. This would not be the only time our Lord's plan would be heard that day.

Yes, being someone who loves to speak and preach, I took the opportunity to give the toast. Since there were roughly 50 people at the service, I made sure everyone was recognized, so I addressed how they had impacted our lives. There were lots of laughs and tears throughout the process. I left the kids until last and thanked them for what they had done for me. This left two more points that needed to be addressed and toasted. Before I toasted my new wife, I had to remind everyone that I must thank my Father in heaven for all he had done. I talked about how I had accepted Him as my personal Savior in 1992 and how he had always answered my prayers in His plan. Keep in mind, I was talking to a predominantly secular crowd, who was not exactly heaped in faith.

Chapter 6 – A Second Chance at Love

What a Great opportunity for me to share the Word!

I did tell the story of my prayer for a Christian woman in my life, as I said earlier in this chapter, but with a twist. I did not plan to do this, but His Spirit certainly moved me. When I came to the part where I finished the prayer, instead of pointing to my bride and calmly saying Beth Williams, I shouted, "AND BAM!!! BETH WILLIAMS!!"

People jumped and laughed. I believe the spirit moved them every bit as much as my yell! Everyone in attendance, Christian or non-believers, were fully aware of what my Father and Savior had done to bring us together for ourselves and for our families. That folks, is the Power of Prayer! I then went on to toast and thank my Beth for what she meant to me and my family. They all knew she had so positively and powerfully impacted my life. This was my amazing Christian wife with whom He had so blessed me. I relayed the stories of 43 years ago, when I first met her and how I still felt that excitement every time I see her to this day.

You need to know that He does have a plan for each of us. You will not always understand why and want to follow your own ways. We all do. Never lose your faith or trust in our Father because it is through His grace that we are forgiven over and over again. We don't feel worthy of his blessings, but He still provides it to us if we come in prayer and faith.

Trust in the LORD with all your heart and lean not on your own understanding; in all your ways submit to him, and he will make your paths straight.
Proverbs 3:5-6

Chapter 6 – A Second Chance at Love

Beth and I are building our life together with our five kids and three grandchildren. We are very much in love and so blessed. We give Him all the glory for His blessings, forgiveness and His Son, Our Savior, Jesus Christ.

He is Faithful!!!

- ARTHUR BRITE

Chapter 6 – A Second Chance at Love

About the Author – Arthur Brite

Arthur Brite has been involved in the medical industry since 1980 as a sales representative, sales manager, national sales trainer and is nationally recognized as one of the leading corporate speakers in the medical field. He has won numerous awards for his sales performance, management and training. Arthur is an author, interview expert and a national/international keynote speaker who has spoken all over the world with his message of proven success. He has been a national radio talk show host and conducts national radio interviews regarding his proven formula for winning.

Chapter 6 – A Second Chance at Love

Arthur Brite brings his 4C's method of success, combined with his 34 years of experience in the medical industry to **Bring Out the Extraordinary** in all. His presentation is dynamic, passionate, humorous and educational as he shows how to apply his proven principles. He has spoken to large and small corporations along with medical practices throughout the country to show the importance of creating a winning atmosphere to any product, service or business. Arthur Brite's unique presentations provide a clear direction utilizing stories, career application, and audience participation while making everyone feel important in building for success.

OFFICE ADDRESS: Arthur Brite Enterprises
1598 Arbor Drive
Willoughby, OH 44094
OFFICE TELEPHONE: (440)554-2541
TWITTER: @arthurbrite
EMAIL: arthur@arthurbrite.com
WEBSITE: www.arthurbrite.com
PHONE APP: https://arthurbrite.appsme.com

Chapter 6 – A Second Chance at Love

"Never lose your faith or trust in our Father because it is through His grace that we are forgiven over and over again. We don't feel worthy of his blessings, but He still provides it to us if we come in prayer and faith."
- Arthur Brite

Chapter 6 – A Second Chance at Love

Chapter 7

Living a Balanced Life
By Albert Castillo - California

Many people talk about living, or trying to live, a balanced life.

Over the years, I have listened to co-workers, friends and family discuss life balance and share their views and frustrations. It was clear that many of us struggle with living a balanced life, so during the conversations I started asking the following questions:

What does living a balanced life mean to you? How do you measure it? What are you doing to achieve it?

Personally, I found myself thinking about living a "balanced life," not out of the blue or out of a desire to be balanced, but out of necessity. Like most men I learn a lot about myself from my wife. Sometimes I don't like what I hear, but during those quiet moments of self-reflection, the ugly truth comes out. I realize...dang, she was right, AGAIN. (However, I rarely admitted it, of course.)

Chapter 7 – Living a Balanced Life

My early definition of a balanced life was to do whatever I wanted to do, whenever I wanted to do it. Therefore, to me, I was happy and balanced. As a result, I spent my early years working too much and playing with friends too much. Then, being a hard-headed and determined person, it took several LIFE lessons (and years) to understand the REAL meaning of living a balanced life.

You see, I´m a very driven person. However, I used to only focus my energy on one thing at a time. Then, I would get easily distracted and focus on something else. It was kind of like the cartoons of a dog chasing a ball, seeing a squirrel, forgetting about the ball, and chasing the squirrel again. My wife, Auda, says I have OCD (Obsessive Compulsive Disorder). When I get into something, man I really get into it, so much that whatever I´m into at the moment gets my complete focus. I tune out everything else, (meaning her, at least that's how she used to describe it). At first, I thought this was a good thing.

My response used to be, *Do you remember when you were a kid playing with a magnifying glass? What happened when you focused the sun's energy through the glass onto a paper object? Boom, instant fire.* That was me, focused and on fire…or so I thought.

My objective is to share with you just a few of my life lessons from living an unbalanced life, what I've learned and how I´ve turned the table to become balanced (at least most of the time).

Chapter 7 – Living a Balanced Life

Lesson #1 (Relationships - Workplace)

Meeting and getting to know new people is an enjoyable experience for me.

In doing so, I have found that there are many unhappy work-life warriors. Nigel Marsh was right in saying there are thousands of people working at jobs they hate, for people they don't like, earning money to buy things they don't need in order to impress people they don't like!

Like most people, early in my professional career, I was out to make a name for myself. While my degree is in engineering, I quickly found out I didn't like sitting at a desk working on engineering drawings or crunching numbers on my calculator all day. Maybe I didn't like it because they told me I talked too much. In either case, I took my talents into technical sales. My goal was to win every sales contest. I had a whatever-it-takes attitude, willing to work long, hard hours figuring out ways to beat everyone else.

I quickly found out that competing was tough from 8-5, but after five or before eight was when my efforts paid off best. During those times, my strategy was simply to do things others weren't willing to do to succeed! My strategy worked. I won many sales contests and always placed in the top five in an organization of 200+. What I didn't realize is that I was so competitive that sometimes I treated my fellow co-workers as the competition. As a result, I was not a good team player. There were times when I saw that others were struggling and knew that I could help them, but if I did,

I knew their results would be better or close to mine causing me to work harder to win. So early on, I sometimes pretended not to notice. At first, my boss encouraged me; he saw my energy, enthusiasm, and determination and he liked the results. In the beginning, it drove everyone to work harder and the results were good, but it didn't last long. We became so competitive with each other that we were all working longer and harder than we needed to, but no one was willing to step up and say we needed to stop and work as a team.

Then one day our boss took the team to a "Get Motivated" seminar. There were a few good motivators at the event, but there was one who hit home with all of us; his name was Zig Ziglar. He hit home with us with this one quote: "You can have everything in life you want if you just help enough other people get what they want." That phrase became our team's buzz phrase around the office. We started helping each other, working smarter, having fun and producing great results. The best part was that as a result of our newfound teamwork, we all had a lot more free time to do and enjoy other things besides work.

Whether it's in your job description or not, if you help develop the people you work with, it will actually make your job easier, more fun, and you will build winning relationships.

Chapter 7 – Living a Balanced Life

Lesson #2 (Family Relationships)

Growing up, my mom and dad were very loving and supportive. So family has always been important to me.

There was a time early in our marriage when I used to play competitive tournament softball. I played a lot of sports over the years and baseball/softball was one of my favorites. We had recently purchased a new home and as a result, I made new friends in the area. We started off playing in a recreational softball league once a week. This quickly turned into a competitive tournament travel team playing several times a week plus weekends. On the surface, it doesn't sound bad, but what I forgot to mention is that we had recently become parents (for the first time)…of twin daughters! Surely you can imagine the issues now. When we were playing in the recreational league, my wife would bring the twins in the stroller and stroll around while we played. However, once the competitive travel team started, it wasn't practical for her and the kids to travel, so the conversations about softball soon turned into arguments.

Thinking back as I write this, I remember some of the idiotic things I used to say, like "I have known softball longer than I´ve known you," referring to her asking me to make a choice between her and playing. I was so caught up in the competitiveness of playing and winning that I was spending my family time away from my family. To make matters worse, many of the other dad players were choosing to do the same and so we had another thing in common.

Chapter 7 – Living a Balanced Life

It was a constant internal struggle for me because when I was out playing softball, I was thinking about my wife and kids, as deep down I knew I should be spending time with them. It took me a few years of stubbornness to finally admit this to myself and do the right thing.

I learned several lessons as a result of this turbulent time. First, be careful of the influences of others. If those around you don't have and live the same values as you, naturally there will be misalignment and negative outcomes. That said, it doesn't mean your friends need to be a perfect fit, but it does mean you should be aware of where your values line up and if your interactions are centered on them.

Second, the reality is you need to make friends, career, and other lifestyle choices that are compatible with your current family situation. I have engaged in many conversations where individuals say "If I had the opportunity to do it over…I would have spent more time with my kids when they were young." We all know that we can't turn back the clock, yet we make decisions for short-term personal satisfaction versus life-long enjoyment and fulfillment, and then complain about it later.

Finally, take the time to communicate family values with your spouse. While I love my children and choose to make great sacrifices for them, eventually they will grow up and have their own families, leaving us as empty-nesters.

The need is not only to focus on raising our kids with a positive mental attitude, with solid Christian values, but also to invest in each other (husband and wife relationship) now, so that we can enjoy the remainder of our post-parenting lives in harmony together.

Lesson #3 (Financial Prosperity)

Financial prosperity always seems to be a big topic during conversations. Sometimes people engage in the conversation just to compare how much they make to others. Other times people want to know how to make more money. I have learned that most people have not thought out exactly what financial prosperity means to them. Most don't know their personal financial number, why the number is important, what sacrifices they are willing to make to hit their number, and what they will do when they reached it.

I started working at a young age. Zig Ziglar said "I've had money and haven't had it, and YES it's better to have it." Rita Davenport said "Money isn't everything… but it ranks right up there with oxygen!" We have all heard Zig say "Many people say money won't solve your problems, but it sure seems like everyone wants to find out for themselves."

I have had the opportunity to be among some financially prosperous individuals. In order to calibrate the topic, my definition of financially prosperous individuals are those in excess of 10 Million net worth. In many of the cases, it seems that those who made an extraordinary amount of money lost their family, health, or friends in the process. Most were on their second marriage, or just as sad, did not spend much time with their children while they were growing up.

Chapter 7 – Living a Balanced Life

They sacrificed their family in order to achieve financial wealth and most of them regret it.

Personally, I get it. I like nice things too and always prefer quality over quantity. However, just as much as I enjoy buying nice things for myself, I enjoy buying nice things for my kids and especially for my wife. This also keeps me in good standing with her and as the saying goes, "Happy wife, happy life."

In my case, I enjoy being a provider. I learned that from my dad, so being able to provide is what drives me. My dad is a very hard worker and old school, so he wanted my mom to spend the necessary time taking care of my brother and me. He would do what was necessary to provide for us. As a result, I learned that what drove me to *work and earn* was my fundamental desire to provide for my family. Also, knowing that I am a compulsive person, I had to grow very aware and learn to listen to my wife, so that I could keep in balance. After all, if the real reason for working is to provide, and I lose my wife and kids in the process, then what is the point, right?

Today, we still have a target financial number and we review it together annually. When those tough times come (and they often do), we make a decision together on the sacrifices that need to be made in order to raise our financial lid and get closer to our financial target. Our decision is always based on what's best for the family, (not only financially best) with the goal to provide for our children today and leave a lasting legacy for future generations.

Chapter 7 – Living a Balanced Life

One of my favorite quotes is "It's not what you leave for your children…it's what you leave in your children." This is the fundamental consideration of every major financial earning decision we make. So in our minds, if we make a lot of money, but don't spend quality time raising and coaching our children, then we will have failed as parents.

Lesson #4 (Personal Growth)

I define personal development or growth as activities that develop talents, self-awareness, enhance the quality of life, and contribute to the realization of dreams and aspirations. Many things fall into these categories like improving wealth, spiritual development, building employability, and health.

Personal development can also include the developing of other people. This takes place through roles such as those of a coach or mentor. I'm blessed with the opportunity to be able to develop the potential of employees, friends, family, and others through personal relationships or private professional coaching and mentoring. However, in order for me to have the opportunities presented to me today, I had to spend many years developing the skills necessary for my own personal growth. Today, I share in public what I've been practicing in private for years.

It started with me having to give up my blame list. Meaning when things did not go well, I started to blame other things. Things like friends, company policy, government, interest rates, my boss or other team members. It was difficult for me to give up the blame list because that meant it was all on me.

Chapter 7 – Living a Balanced Life

Then one day while listening to Zig Ziglar speak, his word hit me, "It's not what happens to you that determines your future, it's what you do with what happens to you that determines your future." This simple, yet profound statement smacked me across the face and woke me up. Life happens to all of us right? So what was I going to do when it happened next time? Keep blaming others or make changes to alter the outcomes? I slowly started to change my outcomes and my future, by changing me. When I refer to changing me, I'm referring to changing myself on the inside, not the outside.

So, I started changing my mindset. I realized that in order for me to have more I simply had to be more. This was one of my "aha moments!" I adopted the words from Jim Rohn and "Stopped wishing things were easier and started wishing I was better" and I "Stopped wishing for fewer problems and started wishing for more skills to solve more problems." This is now my never-ending adventure, to get better and better at raising my personal lid so that I can raise the lid on countless others.

If you would have known me at age 25, you would have said I'm a hard worker. I'm always early and never hesitate to stay late if needed. I worked hard at my job, but not on myself, and was frustrated sometimes with not earning more money. Once I started working on myself, with the intention of adding more value to those who came in contact with me, my income started to dramatically increase. The harder I worked on myself, the faster the promotions started flowing, along with raises and opportunities from other employers.

Chapter 7 – Living a Balanced Life

I stopped blaming and trying to change things out of my control and let the gifts that God gave me start working for me. I developed (and continue to develop) my personal growth strategy, positive mental attitude, communication, presentation skills, and all the other personal abilities God gave me. As a result, everything started to change for the better. I truly believe if you focus on developing and improving yourself with the intention of adding value to others, you too will have the best results.

Lesson #5 (Spirituality)

I believe that in order to be truly balanced, spirituality should encompass you in all your personal areas of value. I grew up going to Catholic elementary and high school and was an altar boy through middle school. However, as time went on, I became distant from the Catholic Church… until I met my wife.

I say distant because I never felt separated nor denied my faith. However, I certainly did not make the effort to attend mass every Sunday to uphold my religious obligations. I guess you could say I was a fair-weather Catholic. Every time I felt I needed a little help from God, I would pray or swing by the church to light a candle and spend time asking for his helping hand and guidance.

As a side note, have you ever noticed how people who say they don't believe in God, start praying for help when they are desperate or in a life-changing situation? I wasn't quite that bad, but I clearly remember praying for wisdom right before college exams, praying for the safe and healthy birth of my children, praying for quick recovery from injuries, and the list goes on and on.

In short, I was living my life by sight and not by faith. If I could see it, I would believe it. My wife was really the one who started to turn this around for me. After we got married, I underestimated her faith. She too was raised a Catholic. However, she never strayed. She was strong and consistent in her beliefs that we needed to live a faith-filled life. Early on it was an uphill battle for her, as I didn't feel the same way at first. I kept telling her mass was boring for me; when we were there I found myself thinking about other things. However, once our twin daughters were born something just clicked inside me. All the things my wife had been saying about living a faith-filled life and raising a family embracing Christianity finally made sense. Like all parents, we wanted the best for our children.

Then my wife hit me right in the heart when she said "When we are not around and your daughters need a little support and guidance, who do you want them to turn to? A complete stranger or God?" That was it, DONE DEAL, I was ALL IN. With her help, I began to embrace my religious roots again, revisiting and re-learning everything taught to me in elementary and high school. My life took on new meaning and I started to live a life of servanthood .

When I finally turned the corner and started my path serving him, all of a sudden I had clarity, and all aspects of my life started leading towards abundance. I truly feel I have been and continue to be blessed.

Chapter 7 – Living a Balanced Life

Even though I have not held up my end of the bargain with God, he has unconditionally been there for me. I certainly owe all that I have to him: great family relationships, good friends, peace of mind, reasonably prosperous, good health, and great hope for the future.

Believe in him, his love for all of us is unconditional. Embrace him in all areas and aspects of your life. Live a life of servanthood and you too will share in his grace and glory!

In Summary:
- If you want to achieve a higher level of productivity and effectiveness, it requires living a balanced life. When you achieve balance of your core values, you will live a balanced life that is sustainable and you will be successful in all areas.
- Whether you're single, married or in a serious relationship, create balance with the things that matter most to you.
- Frequently (more in the beginning) evaluate yourself and have your spouse or loved one evaluate you as well. An external view from someone you trust is important.
- Understand there will be transitions/seasons in life that will require more focus in certain areas than others (single to married, married to married with kids, starting a new business). You will need to spend a little more time in some areas than others.

Chapter 7 – Living a Balanced Life

That's okay, you will quickly identify when you need to refocus on neglected areas.

Put God first. My view is that when you put Him first, He will encompass everything that is important to you. Ultimately, He is the one who holds you and everything about you together.

- Albert Castillo

Chapter 7 – Living a Balanced Life

About the Author – Albert Castillo

Albert Castillo has more than 20 years of experience as a leader, coach, and mentor. Through a broad range of personal and professional life experiences, he has grown a passion for developing others and helping them be the best they can be. He strives to live out his life´s purpose by adding value to his family, friends, and colleagues. Albert finds great fulfillment, from building winning relationships to enjoying networking, in an effort to connect leaders and business people worldwide.

Chapter 7 – Living a Balanced Life

He is a student in the game of life, constantly developing others, while continuously looking to improve himself. Albert is a Ziglar Legacy Certified trainer and is also certified by John Maxwell as an Advanced Global Executive Leadership coach and trainer.

Albert believes everyone is born to win, and that living a balanced, faith-driven life is the key to success in all facets of your life.

Albert and his amazing wife of 20 years, Auda, have three beautiful daughters: Alyssa, Alina, Alyiah, and a handsome dog Apollo. They reside in Los Angeles, California. When Albert is not leading, he enjoys traveling and spending time with his wife, as well as watching his daughters train and compete in sports.

Albert can be contacted by email at: ateam17@hotmail.com

Chapter 7 – Living a Balanced Life

"Believe in him, his love for all of us is unconditional.
Embrace him in all areas and aspects of your life.
Live a life of servanthood and you too will
share in his grace and glory!"
Albert Castillo

Chapter 8 – Goodbye, Mr. Mediocrity

Chapter 8

Goodbye, Mr. Mediocrity
By Daniel Collins - St. Maarten

August 18, 2011, started like so many days before, yet by the end of that day my life and the lives of my immediate family would be changed forever. I arrived to work a little before 8:00 a.m. and got right down to the essentials, starting with a complete breakfast. I needed to get fueled up for what was to happen. As soon as I arrived, my manager called me into his office. He told me that I would need to meet with top management for the company before I signed on to my computer. He explained that it would be a very tough meeting and that I should prepare myself.

A few weeks prior, I had already met with the company security department because a matter was being investigated, and they needed to ask me a few questions. Soon afterwards, I was called by a local detective who requested a meeting with me as well. I soon realized that this was a serious matter so, I decided that I needed to call a few people. Whenever I have situations that are disturbing or troublesome there are four people that I talk to:

Chapter 8 – Goodbye, Mr. Mediocrity

The first is God because He is always available and His answers will never be wrong. I also speak to my wife, of course, who may not always understand what is going on or even how to deal with it, but she has proven to be a great support. The other people I speak to are my mother and my pastor. My mother may have more questions than answers at times, but I can always count on her to be a prayer warrior. My pastor is also a prayer warrior and an extremely wise counselor. I've known Pastor Webster since 2004 and he has never given me, or those around me, bad advice. As a final step, I prayed in my pickup truck before returning to the office.

Now fortified, I told my manager that I called some folks and prayed. His demeanor had not changed from our previous conversation that morning. He was troubled. I could see it on his face and hear it in his voice. He reminded me that it was going to be a tough meeting and to maintain my composure.

A few minutes later, I arrived at the conference room at the main office which was located about five minutes away by foot. At this meeting were the managing director, the manager of human resources, the legal counsellor, the manager of my department, and me, of course. Soon after the discussion started, it became clear that it would be my last day employed by the company and that I would need to leave. The only question I had to answer was: How would I leave? Would I resign or would I be suspended, followed by them seeking termination? I made my decision, signed what they had prepared, then left.

Chapter 8 – Goodbye, Mr. Mediocrity

My manager asked for me to leave quietly and not to mention anything to the staff, which was a good idea. Mentioning anything would have only led to a multitude of questions and emotions and besides, management wanted to be first to inform the ones I worked with. I told my colleagues that something came up and that I had to leave. Leaving like this made it a bit easier because saying goodbye to such a great group of people would have been tough. I had spent the previous seven years in that office, formed great relationships along the way, and now life as normal was coming to an abrupt halt.

Out the door I went with no idea what to do or where to go. My phone started ringing and it was my manager. He wanted to let me know that he had a discussion with the other members of management and they agreed to give me some additional time to make up my mind; they felt that I didn't get much time to think the decision through. With these additional hours on hand, I called my pastor and asked for an urgent meeting. He wasn't at home, but where he was proved to be the ideal place for me to think clearly about making such a life-altering decision.

As we sat there discussing my present and my future, we considered all options, while looking out over the Caribbean Sea. It was a sunny day with calm, tropical breezes and birds chirping in the background. Airplanes would pass by interrupting the quietness ever so often. Contrasting the beautiful day was the turbulence I was trying to deal with. If I didn't have a job, how could I take care of my wife and two children? How would the bills get paid?

Chapter 8 – Goodbye, Mr. Mediocrity

Less than one year prior, my wife started working, so our income would not fall to zero, but how would I fill the gap? Throughout my visit, Pastor Webster was completely calm on the outside, although I had no idea what was going on inside his head. He asked the key questions that helped me make the right choice. The most important question was: If you chose not to resign, but to fight this matter, how sure are you that your employer would not be able to hold anything against you? I thought for a while and could not conclude that there wasn't anything they could hold against me. They had already leveled allegations, which, though they were untrue, I could not disprove them. Instead of a long, drawn out battle that I was not guaranteed to win, I chose to resign that day. I prepared and delivered my resignation letter to the managing director. He accepted it, barely looking at me in the process. They did make sure that my payout would be equivalent to three months income, so for the next few months, we would not starve.

In order to avoid having to explain rumors to my parents, my wife and I decided to visit them that evening. I told them what had happened, the details, and what my current situation was. The truth is that fraud was committed by another employee. I was not at fault, I was not aware of the fraud, nor did I benefit from it. This information did not stop the key ladies in my life from being upset, my mother especially. If she had gotten close to the perpetrator she would have had some choice words for her and maybe some ninja moves, too.

So now what do you do when morning comes, you are no longer employed, and have nothing to do? Answer: you go to the beach.

Chapter 8 – Goodbye, Mr. Mediocrity

I got ready that morning, we dropped the children off at school, I dropped my wife off at work, and I went to the beach. This time, it was almost at the extreme opposite end of the island where I went to speak to my pastor the day before.

From my location, I could look out over the Atlantic Ocean, which, quite like my situation, was very turbulent. It was very different from the calm I experienced the years before in my job and very different from the view I had 24 hours earlier while sitting with my pastor and looking over the Caribbean Sea. I spent my time there on that beach in a lot of prayer. I listened to the messages of the Christian preacher on the radio station in my truck. I don't remember what was said, but at that point I sought encouragement everywhere, and thanks to many people around me, I found it.

What else do you do when you have nothing to do? You keep yourself busy. How? At church. In hindsight, it almost looked like I lost my job just in time to spend my days at our church assisting Pastor Webster. During the third quarter of 2011, we were in the final stages of rebuilding our worship center. It was crunch time and we needed all hands on deck. My main job was to find whatever we needed to order, work out the best deal, and get it to the island on time. Whether it was projectors from New York, a generator from Miami, signage from Ohio, or lightbulbs from Holland, I just had to find the best deal and get them to the island on time. At this point, I learned that I had to keep myself busy, which kept me from hosting pity parties for myself.

During this period, my greatest fear was *"What would my former colleagues think about me?"*

Chapter 8 – Goodbye, Mr. Mediocrity

This was significant because I needed to find another job, and if my reputation was tarnished, then it would have been very difficult to find another job. The establishment I left was large with over 200 employees and had been around for more than 45 years. One thing was for sure, I had learned from a friend, some years before that in order to be up, you need to dress up.

In other words, I made sure that wherever I went, I was neatly attired and that my clothes were well ironed. I was representing God and he wouldn't want me looking shabby.

Be careful what you pray for, you might just get it.

In 2010, the year before, I had been chosen as father of the year. One of the gifts I received was a trip to a spiritual growth conference. Pastor Webster had already been attending a conference held in Dallas, Texas by Dr. Tony Evans. I was fortunate to bring my wife on this free trip. We enjoyed the experience and benefited greatly from the things we learned.

Now in 2011, my pastor once again reminded us about the conference and told us to encourage others to go; those others included my relatives. We did not have the money budgeted for this trip, so we prayed early that year for God to provide the funds to travel to the conference if it was His will for us to go. All of a sudden I had no job, but I had more than enough money to pay for the trip and all the related costs to experience this conference. I discussed it with my wife and we agreed that since God provided the answer to our prayer and the money for the trip that we should use the money for the purpose we had prayed for.

Chapter 8 – Goodbye, Mr. Mediocrity

Of course, others had different ideas on how we should use the money. Some said, "You shouldn't go! Save all the money you can at this point!" I believe God tests us from time to time to see if we really trust Him to provide for us. I wanted to keep as much money as possible, for as long as possible, but we decided to trust God and go.

We made all the arrangements and booked the trip for me, my wife, my mother-in-law, and my sister-in-law.

The experience was great, especially knowing how God had provided and that if my wife and I did not go, neither my mother-in-law nor my sister-in-law would have gone. To this day, Pastor Webster still recalls that conference as the turning point. This was especially true for my mother-in-law, who found her area of service in the work of the Lord and immersed herself in it. Looking back, it is still amazing how God allowed me to lose that job and provided an answer to prayer all at the same time.

How do you know what to do?

For years, I would look at my career, which was spent in the areas of economics and finance, and I would try to find where I was making a difference. I compared myself to people in construction, who could point at a bridge or building and say, "That was not there before I started, now, after my hard work, there it stands." I knew that I was not making a difference and was searching to do something significant with my life. Wanting to make a difference made me picky in choosing the next job. I was not willing to accept another regular 8-to-5 job because not working a regular job

Chapter 8 – Goodbye, Mr. Mediocrity

allowed me to be much more involved with my wife and children. After some months, there was only one organization that had a proper response to my queries for a job, and it was in sales (life insurance sales) based on pure commission. A dream come true? Not really.

Now, nobody I spoke to, thought I could sell: not my wife, not my mother, not my pastor and not even I thought I could sell. However, I was willing to give it a try. I started training late 2011 and started selling by January 2012. Being in sales quickly forced me to grow in the areas of goal setting, time management or priority management, listening skills, interpersonal skills, and self-motivation, among other skills.

My first year went well and by September of that same year, I was advisor of the month. During our staff Christmas party, I was given a book on sales, *The Little Red Book of Selling* by Jeffrey Gitomer. Although the content of Gitomer's book gave good sales information and other helpful material, I found his language a bit too crude so I kept searching.

My search led me to Zig Ziglar and I consumed what he had to offer. I signed up for online training entitled Success 2.0, I got the Born to Win Seminar CD/DVD set, I downloaded podcasts, and turned our cars into automobile universities. I even made a playlist of the various songs sung by The Ziglar Singers. My children love "Mr. Mediocrity."

My courage grew as a salesman and, with it, my confidence, commissions, and bonuses. Then, one day Ziglar offered opportunities to become a certified trainer of their material. I watched the webinar and it was that day that I finally, clearly realized what I was born to do.

Chapter 8 – Goodbye, Mr. Mediocrity

I got my answer to why I was on this planet. I had to get certified, it was a must, but how do you set aside all the money needed for the certification? I had to pay for the training, flight, accommodation, transportation, meals, and shopping. How could I pay for this? It was thousands of dollars.

Although I was growing as a salesman, we were only barely getting through the months.

We worked out plans, brainstormed, and prayed. I didn't have the money and it didn't look like I would get it anytime soon. Now in the meantime, we had also been listening to Dave Ramsey and found out that our money needed a total makeover. This made us willing to sell things in order to get financially fit. Our credit card was paid off and canceled, along with the truck loan we had, and we also had a small emergency fund going.

One day, I had the brilliant idea to sell the truck, which would bring in enough money to cover all related costs of certification. Now I loved this truck, and my wife and children loved this truck, too. To this day, if we see the truck anywhere, we would have an ad hoc moment of silence. It was a 2006 Chevrolet Colorado, Blue, Crew Cab, four-wheel drive, 3.5 liter, 5-cylinder truck. I hand-picked this truck about three years prior. So, I ran the idea by my wife and she said, "But, you love that truck!" Despite the difficulty for her to part with it, she was OK with it. We also prayed about it and got busy immediately. I printed the for-sale signs and posted it on social media too.

Chapter 8 – Goodbye, Mr. Mediocrity

I didn't get any serious offers until one day I went to start the truck and the battery was dead. Now, the last thing I wanted to do was to spend more money on a truck that I was selling. Not too excited, I jump-started the truck and went to buy a replacement battery. I parked and left the motor running, and there he was, coming out of the same store I was going into. It was the new owner of my truck.

We got down to negotiating, and in the end, the exact amount we wanted and prayed for, we got. I am reminded of the portion of scripture found in James 4:2 which states: ***"...Yet you do not have because you do not ask." (NKJV)***
God has so much in store for us that we will never enjoy because we do not ask.

It was a Saturday that we agreed to sell the truck and it was sold by Monday afternoon. Now this was hurdle number one that God helped us cross. I could not wait to get on the line with Ziglar, and after contacting them, I found out that the upcoming class should have been full, but two people had dropped out. Hurdle two crossed.

Certification went great and I met some wonderful people while there. On July 18th, 2014, I got my biggest takeaway, which was me coming to the realization that all my life I had been mediocre. Maybe that's why my children liked the song "Mr. Mediocrity" so much. I usually did just enough to get by, just enough to pass the exam, just enough not to get fired, just enough not to starve. I tried to explain this in front of the class through tears; I think they got it. You may not know me, but I was not a public crier, I wasn't even a private crier,

Chapter 8 – Goodbye, Mr. Mediocrity

but I had to be truthful that day and admit to the class and myself that my life, up to that point, was mediocre.

While driving home from the Ziglar office that day, I made a commitment to never be mediocre again. The thing is, we can never truly go forward until we admit where we are and what got us there.

I got into the construction business.

Remember earlier I mentioned that I compared myself to people who were in the construction business? Well, I realized that I needed to get into construction myself. Please understand that I have no plans to erect buildings or bridges or any of the like. I plan to work in the construction of lives, relationships, and organizations. I want to be able to look at people and say to myself, *"I had a positive part to play in that person's life"* or *"Thank God that couple allowed me to sit with them, look how they've grown."*

The power of the written goal.

For years, I had been telling my pastor that he needed to write a book. At least some of his experience, knowledge, and vision needed to be recorded for future generations, according to me. We are presently in the process of starting a Christian school from Kindergarten through University. The strange thing is that a few weeks ago he spoke about a book, but the part he was willing to play was that of a journal keeper. His intention is to make that journal available so the rest of the committee could then write a book after he is gone.

Chapter 8 – Goodbye, Mr. Mediocrity

The strangest thing is that as I was reading my list of current goals that I wrote last August, one of the goals I wrote down was to write a book (or two or three). This goal was dormant for about seven months and only now, has it become relevant again. This written goal is finally coming to life and it makes me wonder what would happen if I reviewed all the goals I wrote down and worked my goal planner to achieve them. I could tell you what would happen: my life and the lives of those around me would dramatically change for the better.

Now, I ask you: What would happen if you took your time to write your goals down, sift through them to determine the ones worth pursuing, complete a goals program, and work on your goals daily? Well, your life would dramatically change for the better, too.

The biggest lesson I've learned from my life is that I am responsible for my life; I can build it or break it. I cannot depend on anyone else to bring me to the level I need to be. My life is my choice and I choose to make it the best life possible. I've spent too many years being mediocre; now I've chosen to be magnificent.
What do you choose?

- Daniel Collins

I thank my wife Latanya who is the only person who chose to be related to me. Sweetness, your support is immeasurable. I also thank everyone whoever gave me an encouraging word.

Chapter 8 – Goodbye, Mr. Mediocrity

About the Author – Daniel Collins

Daniel was born and raised in the Caribbean and presently resides on the island of St. Maarten. Although he spent several years in The Netherlands and a semester in Akron, Ohio, St. Maarten is home and there is no place he'd rather be.

He has spent the last 13 years happily married to his wonderful wife, Latanya and their family also includes two children, a son named Dominick and a daughter named Lael.

Chapter 8 – Goodbye, Mr. Mediocrity

Daniel serves as a deacon at the Good News Baptist Church and keeps himself busy with various responsibilities which include overseeing the youth, finance, and audio-visual departments. He also enjoys teaching classes at church.

Daniel has spent his entire professional career in the Finance and Economics industries. He presently works in sales, which introduced him to one of the greatest salesmen, Zig Ziglar. After studying much of Ziglar's material Daniel got the opportunity to be certified to carry on the Ziglar legacy.

As a Ziglar Legacy Certified trainer, Daniel is now fulfilling his earthly purpose of teaching and training. Through his experience coming from a life of mediocrity, Daniel is now better prepared to assist others in moving from a life that is mediocre to one that is marvelous.

Daniel is determined to grow every day and he is also determined to help others grow too.

You may reach Daniel at:
Email: misterdecollins@gmail.com
Facebook: https://www.facebook.com/myspeakerdaniel

Chapter 8 – Goodbye, Mr. Mediocrity

"I believe God tests us from time to time to see if we really trust Him to provide for us."
Daniel Collins

Chapter 8 – Goodbye, Mr. Mediocrity

Chapter 9

In the Blink of an Eye
By Jason Schmerse - Texas

I consider myself a well-rounded and experienced parent of three boys and four girls. It may matter to some that my four girl children all have four legs, yet to me, they are my children and of course, are treated and respected as such in our home. I make it a point to protect my children the best I can, from all evils and harm in the world. That gets harder in today's technological realm. There is an old humorous saying that if a hammer and duct tape can't fix it, then it's not fixable. In a manner of speaking, the same goes with our children: if we have to wrap our kids in bubble wrap, then there is no point to being a kid. Yet, as an experienced parent, if I were to give advice to any new or expecting parent, I would tell them to expect the worst, buy stock in bubble wrap and send them into the world covered in it. Not really, but it sounds so much less complicated than dealing with the requirements of today's parenting standards.

Parenting should come with its own class in college with books on how to be a counselor, a medic, an auto mechanic to build wooden Boy Scout race cars, a carpenter to repair their furniture, and the list goes on.

Chapter 9 – In the Blink of an Eye

In all my experience as a parent and facing the unexpected in life, I truly wasn't prepared for the phone call of "Your son is being taken by CareFlite to Children's Medical Dallas." Let's take two steps back here and paint the picture leading up to our new-found beginning. Insert workaholic parent, beautiful wife, and three young growing boys. I had a job I loved and felt I did well. I traveled the country working with companies who needed my services to grow their business. I loved the challenge, helping people improve their company and helping them grow. It was important to me to do my job, do it well and ensure my clients were happy with the results of my services. That was my number one priority and where this story begins.

It started with an inevitable paradigm shift that I wouldn't realize until after some soul searching for days and even more weeks after my son's accident. What took me by surprise was the realization that I wasn't truly happy with my life. I needed to re-order my priorities to get back to being the real me and to the happiness I deserved. While the shell of my being appeared and acted happy, on the center stage of life, I wasn't happy. I didn't really even pay attention to that. I was trying so hard to help everyone else, I avoided me and those that should have been important to me. I was holding the wrong values in the wrong order, ending the drought of happiness. I decided to get my priorities in order. I started with renewing my faith by putting God first. Then, with God as my center stage, I renewed my promise to my family. I never changed my work ethic; I was putting the priorities of my faith and my family ahead of my work.

Chapter 9 – In the Blink of an Eye

I knew I needed this adjustment to reach my complete goal of happiness. I periodically go back to the thought of my son's accident and wonder what I could have done to change it for him. However, every time I think of playing the "victim of circumstance" card by trying to correct the past with these thoughts, "Should I have not left town a day early? Should I not have bought my oldest son his bow and arrow set?" I am reminded of my renewed faith and will live purposefully. It's a hard pill to swallow when your child, "your baby," that you strive so hard to provide for and to protect, gets hurt. At the time, even with today's technological advances, there was no clarity as to how bad he was hurt or when we would have answers.

As the story goes, I was Skyping my youngest son Blake and my wife Kelli, as I was on a work trip. The discussion was about how he was upset for tripping and falling on his McDonald's dinner. My oldest son, Nathaniel, bolted into the room to tell my wife that Dylan, my other son, was dying and that she should come quickly. Being a mother of three boys, we could insert the *cry-wolf-tale* here, but in calmness, she went to see what was going on. When she got to Dylan, he wouldn't take his hand off his eye. Kelli noticed there was blood on his face. In a calm voice, she said to me, "Jason, I need to call you back, there's blood." How could I have prepared myself for the call back from my neighbor telling me they were taking my son by CareFlite to Children's Medical Dallas?

Chapter 9 – In the Blink of an Eye

Dylan had taken an arrow to the eye climbing into a large cardboard box. My oldest son thought he was alone in the room when he stabbed the box with his arrow. He never saw Dylan climb in. As Dylan peeked through one of the holes, the blunt tip of the arrow pierced his eye. In the blink of an eye, our lives would be forever changed. Doctors had no way of telling how far the arrow went into the eye or how far back to the brain for that matter. It was a wait-and-see game. Being 800 miles away, I was helpless. Since it was so late, I couldn't even take a flight until the next morning.

When I arrived in Dallas, Dylan was already in surgery. I remember I couldn't even cry, not in the airport nor on the plane, as I was in shock. When I walked into the surgery waiting room and saw Kelli, it broke me. I bawled and told her he's as tough as they come. What she told me in the midst of the most tragic event so far in my life, would set the wheels in motion for me to change. I would become the man I should be, the husband my wife deserved, the father my kids deserved, and the follower Christ deserved. Kelli didn't ask, "Why did this have to happen to our so innocent child?" She did say, "God only gives us what we can handle."

Dylan came out of surgery with seventeen stitches to put the eye back together. We just waited and prayed, not knowing the extent of the damages. I don't think I can pretend to tell you I remember everyone and the show of support from friends, family, and even the community in which we live. I do remember wondering why this child wasn't as important to me as my job was. It hurts to say that out loud even now,

Chapter 9 – In the Blink of an Eye

and it's not as if I neglected my children, not even close. I provided for them, spent time with them riding four-wheelers and taking them to Rangers baseball games. We made memories. However, as I looked back to my childhood and my upbringing, my father's core center was his relationship with God. It was less of spoiling me and my brother and more of building our character. He was shaping us to be Godly men with a purpose, yet, having fun in the process.

As Dylan was lying helpless in a hospital bed, I remember hearing the day before the accident about an invention. This invention could send digital images to the brain that one can see from the eye. Would this be what we had to look forward to with my son losing his eye? The eye is the only organ in the human body you cannot transplant. A second surgery was needed to allow doctors to better look into the eye and reveal the extent of the damages. An ultrasound on the eye proved that the eye was actually good. However, it was explained to us that it was like a shaken egg; everything inside was jumbled. Further tests were needed to know if he would ever see more than light and shadows. Days would ensue before Dylan would be walking around the hospital clutching his transformers blanket and bumblebee transformer toy. He was proving that no one could knock him down for long. Then came the light test and with it, one of the hardest decisions I have ever had to make for my child.

Should he keep his eye or should it be removed? It wasn't without a lot of research and prayer to ease our decision for

Chapter 9 – In the Blink of an Eye

our child's future. There was a chance that our son could see more than light and shadows. However, the stinger was that there was a four percent chance that our son would lose vision in his good eye as the body tried to repair the bad eye. Four percent doesn't sound like a large probability until you think your son will be completely blind, then that number becomes astronomical. To continue down the path of difficulties for my son, this decision to remove his eye had to be made within two days. Waiting any longer would initiate a risk of the body beginning to repair. This would create a chance of harm to the good eye.

The decision was made. He would have to consider himself a transformer with a prosthetic glass eye. All I could think of is, "Where is that bubble wrap for my son that I promise he will be wrapped in from here on out?"

A few weeks went by and I had to go back to work. I began the process of setting the goal to reorder my life, but where would I begin? My perception of my life modification was based on how people saw me physically. As a result, I needed to lose weight. The reality of this kicked in when I decided to get Ziglar Legacy Certified. During one class, there was a wheel with spokes on it that outlined a lack of balance in my life. As I aligned all those key attributes and set goals to turn my life around, it was clear that my spiritual spoke needed to be adjusted first. From there all would begin to fall into place.

My renewed faith led me to success in my personal life and further success in my business life.

Chapter 9 – In the Blink of an Eye

I'm naturally a very happy and outgoing person. However, when I tell people I'm happier now than I have ever been before, I get the *"How is that even possible"* look. I stopped focusing on what I thought people wanted to see from me and started focusing on my faith. Happiness wasn't my issue, I felt happy in a way, I just wasn't balanced.

I became closer to my wife and we became ironically enough, better friends and a closer couple. I became closer to my children too. I didn't even know what I was missing until I slowed down to become more involved in their lives. Nathaniel, my oldest son, and I are enjoying our ski time more and dirt-bike riding more. He even enjoys when I take him to work with me from time to time. It took some time after the accident to get Dylan out from under the wing of his mother, but he is back to being his active self. He's not shy about his "fake" eye and as of yet, he doesn't take it out to show the girls. I truly believe my youngest son Blake has seen the results of my transformation the most. We now have a bond we never had before. We can just talk for hours (maybe a little wrestling in between). When we are together I feel like, to him, it's just me and dad. I treasure…No, I cherish this.

People ask me, "How does renewing your faith affect your business life?" My response is, "I am blessed with the relationships I have forged in my line of work. I truly believe God has placed people in my business life for a reason. Now, every relationship I have made has fostered into a meaningful bond.

Chapter 9 – In the Blink of an Eye

In my past, I have only shared this with a few business relationships."

I was at a business event when a challenge was brought to my attention that would stick with me to this day. The task was to name a successful multi-millionaire: actor, actress, singer, male/female or a famous businessman/woman that are pronounced atheist. The stipulation was that they could not be affiliated with a religious group. This sets the stage that in order to be successful; your foundation should start with God.

I've never had a roadmap to my life, I have always adapted and gone down the path or highway that seemed most fitting at the time. As my walk takes me closer to God, it has afforded me absolutes in the fact that my challenges in life are most likely small rivals. I now rethink, re-look, and re-purpose my life to be the man, the husband, the father, the friend, and the example I am today. While I would love to look back on my life and say I was a happy and God-fearing man, the best husband, father and friend I could have been, I can only reiterate my renewed faith. This new faith is due to a tragedy that has helped me triumph in my walk with God.

Life's challenges are a given; overcoming is a choice. If you ever think of how your life can be any different with a closer walk with God, take a different view. Close one eye and see for yourself what it is like to be someone who lost an eye and see the world the way they do.

Chapter 9 – In the Blink of an Eye

Don't feel sorry for them because they have lost depth perception or range of view, yet rejoice with them that they are still able to see and still able to wake in the morning. Rejoice with them that they are past their challenges, trials, and tribulations.

One of my favorite verses is Romans 8:18 "For I consider that the sufferings of this present time are not worth comparing with the glory that is to be revealed to us." (ESV)
- Jason Schmerse

About The Author – Jason Schmerse

Jason Schmerse was born in Janesville, Wisconsin and grew up in a small town, Richmond, Massachusetts. He moved to

Chapter 9 – In the Blink of an Eye

Waxahachie, Texas, and currently resides in both Texas and Colorado with his bride Kelli and three young boys Nathaniel, Dylan, and Blake. They also have four, four-legged girls: Gabby, Khloe, Bumble Bee, and Bella.

Jason attributes his success to his family for helping him keep his focus on God, family, and work. This allows him to work and play hard to keep the balance.

Jason has been a self-proclaimed entrepreneur and small business enthusiast for 15 years. If you haven't seen his television show yet, then you're not alone. However, stay tuned, one might be coming in the distant future. (Insert chuckle here.)

A graduate of Texas Tech University, Jason molded his career from computer programming and project management of Information Technology in the telecommunications industry and was part of a group of pioneers who brought the telephone bill to the World Wide Web. His job was outsourced after 9/11, which forced his hand at becoming an entrepreneur in the Janitorial and Cleaning and Restoration Industries. He has since staged himself as a consultant to help others start or transform their business into elite business platforms.

Jason Schmerse is also a "ZLC" Ziglar Legacy Certified trainer and speaker, and in his spare time enjoys helping troubled teens refine their lives back to the right path to ensure a successful future.

www.facebook.com/eagleeyeperformancesolutions
email: jason.eagleeyeperformance@gmail.com

Chapter 9 – In the Blink of an Eye

"Life's challenges are a given; overcoming is a choice."
Jason Schmerse

Chapter 9 – In the Blink of an Eye

Chapter 10

Bits of Hope
By Nathan Riddle - Texas

This story can be summarized in a quote by Dusty Rhodes, who is also called *The American Dream:* "I have wined and dined with kings and queens, and slept in alleys and dined on pork and beans." Obviously, a quote by a professional wrestler from the eighties is a strange place to begin, but that quote is the essence of life. Life gives the good and bad, and it is best to learn some things on the way. As an example, one conversation I had, began with "Nathan, buddy, I'll just get to it as there is no easy way to do this. I've decided not to renew your contract for next year." That was a soul-crushing defeat. That conversation was followed by several months of "work purgatory," working out a contract, but not really doing anything. Soon my life consisted of sitting at a desk in an office, with a computer, and no real assignment. I shared the office with some very caring people, who did their best to help me get through. There were days when the thought went through my mind, *if I unfasten my seatbelt, peg the gas, and turn into the barrier going over a hundred, this testing will be over.* Having recently purchased my dream car, I knew how fast it could go and it could be a death machine if needed. There were days when I would get angry and go to lunch for three hours. The people in the office would express rightful

Chapter 10 – Bits of Hope

concern. Looking back at that time and reading emails that were sent, I now realize that dark places are dark places and spending long periods in a dark place makes life difficult and sad. However, the world did not stop spinning during this season, life continued and the sun continued to come up on a daily basis. That is the place where these bits of hope come from.

The Prompting
My nephew graduated from High School and was leaving for college. This was an amazing occasion and the whole family was proud.

The guys in the family decided to do an old southern tradition for my nephew. This tradition is known as the Cigar Send-off. In the south, men gather, smoke rare old cigars, sip brandy, and take the time to give the graduate who is off to college some advice. This old tradition is part of becoming a man. We are Baptists, so there had to be changes in the tradition that took place. In the place of cigars were steaks and sausages. In the place of Brandy, we did Shenanigans in the swimming pool. It's amazing to watch grown men in excess of 250-350 lbs. do belly flops and flips into a pool. Somebody brought hummus and a vegetable plate. I'm pretty sure that was a joke because nobody touched the hummus, carrots, or broccoli. Given the option, in general, men will choose meat over vegetables every time. We spent about an hour in the pool doing massive flips, dunks, and playing games, one of which involved a foam football, sometimes sopped full like a sponge. One squeezes a foam football underwater, and then fills it. Said football, now full of water, weighs five to ten pounds.

Chapter 10 – Bits of Hope

Throwing it at a sibling can result in massive pain. Then, it becomes a guessing game. Will this hurt or not? Can I get to the football and retaliate? (Do not try this at home.) We set about breaking every rule of every public pool ever encountered growing up: no running, do not push people in, no animals in the pool, and do not bring food into the pool. (Gross, I know.)

Then we sat down, had cake, and drank a Coke. (In Texas, everything is Coke.) My other nephews were in their late twenties. I was in my late thirties. My brothers were in their forties. My brother-in-law was in his fifties and my father in his sixties. There were five decades of life experiences, and different life stages sitting around the table.

We started giving advice, some simple. If you like a girl, go to her and say something along the lines of: "I think you're interesting, would you like to grab coffee after class tomorrow." "Be confident, upfront, and don't play games." Then we got deeper, and deeper. Not too intense, as heartburn was setting in. So there was no advice on setting up a 401K or anything that deep. As we talked, we discovered there wasn't a whole lot of difference in what we said from person to person. We all felt the same way and there was a lot of "I agree," and "What he said." In the end, we gave out four pieces of advice also known as the bits of hope.

The four pieces of advice were simple:
1. Do not let anyone tell you that you can't do anything.
2. Be yourself.
3. Do the work.
4. Hard times will come, but they don't last.

Chapter 10 – Bits of Hope

These four statements are more than all one needs in this world.

Do not let anyone tell you that you can't do something.

We were fearfully and wonderfully made. The Bible says so in Psalms.

There is not anything that we cannot do, within reason. As a forty-one-year-old man who has never played basketball in my life and stretches to be 5'10", I will not be playing professional basketball.

Our world tears people down, yet we are all endowed by a creator with abilities and skills. The greatest issue we face is listening to the person who lives in our head. People exploit that, and keep us from our greatest potential.

Personally, I grew up poor. We were not, "tin-shack, sleep-on-the-street, walking-in-the-snow five-miles-to-go-to-school-both-ways" poor. However, we were poor. There were times when I got into trouble for having an afternoon snack when dinner was planned. There just wasn't enough peanut butter for the number of days we had to eat. My mom made shorts that I wore. Sometimes, I had to wear shorts underneath my pants because the holes were too large in inappropriate places.

One day, I got a particularly strange call to the front office of the school. When I arrived at the front office, the secretary said, "Your parents called, you need to walk home right away." This was before Ferris Bueller had exploited Principal Rooney to get Sloan out of school, so I was sent home. When

Chapter 10 – Bits of Hope

I arrived, there were three pickups in front of the house and a moving truck. My dad met me at the door with, "You need to pack a bag of clothes, and pack everything else up for storage." My family was separated into three houses of church members. My brothers went to two different homes. My sister, her children, my parents and I lived with another family. Would it not have been for those members of the church, we would have been homeless in the traditional sense. After a week, we moved into another house that was rented from a connection at our church. I would love to say that everything was happy from that point on, but it wasn't. My dad didn't have a full-time job for six years after that. Life was hard. These were defeats for my family. We went from having family dinner every night at a fully set table to having dinner on our own in a kitchen that could only handle a card table. Our clothes washer was in the kitchen, the dryer was just outside the back door.

We were fearfully and wonderfully made. The Bible says so in Psalms.

Eventually, there was a moment. That moment that changed everything for my family. It happened one night toward the end of eighth grade. The three boys, my mom, and dad were at the dinner table. My mother announced, "Guys what we're doing isn't working. I went and enrolled at the college today." This sentence changed the world for our family. My dad was soon a semester behind in the belief that he too could get a college education. One parent had decided not to listen to what the world had been saying to her for the last twenty-five years. The lies that it was too late to go to college didn't have an effect on her anymore.

Chapter 10 – Bits of Hope

She drove to the college campus and discovered that they would allow her in even if society had told her it was twenty-five years too late.

One time a teacher in high school announced at a parent's meeting. "I don't care who you are, if you are a college student, a college professor, or a Pulitzer Prize-winning playwright. You are all parents to us." That was fine to my friend whose dad was a professor. That was fine with the girl whose dad wrote plays for a living. My parents were insulted a little. However, they kept going because they were not going to let anyone allow them to quit.

We were fearfully and wonderfully made. The Bible says so in Psalms.

Today, the poor family lives in a nice house. Being a fan of the UFC, a few years ago my brother said to me, "We should go to a fight in Las Vegas." My thought process was still, *I can't do that, I'm poor.* However, when we researched it, the trip was well within our budget. We went to a prize fight, saw a couple of shows, watched a football game, and had a great time. There had to be a mental shift before we did it.

What if the Wright Brothers had listened to the world, and only ran their bicycle shop? There were engineering and aeronautical specialists, who were working on understanding and obtaining flight at the time. They would have eventually created an airplane. However, those experts are now lost to history. Visiting the Smithsonian Museum today, you can see the Wright Flyer. It is a testament to people who chose not to listen to the world around them.

Chapter 10 – Bits of Hope

We were fearfully and wonderfully made. The Bible says so in Psalms.

Recently, I sat in a room and heard a man in tears say, "No one ever believed in me until I was already an adult." I can't say that about my parents. They have always believed in and helped us to strive for something bigger and better in our lives. That made a world of difference. We were taught to not let people tell us we couldn't.

Be yourself
It's a cliché, right? It can't be that simple. Yes, it is, we were all put on this earth for a reason.

Where would the world be if any random artist decided to not be an artist? What would the New York harbor look like without Bartholdi? (He created the Statue of Liberty.) What would the world of comic books be like if Stan Lee had been an accountant? (He was the creative force behind the majority of Marvel Comic Book characters.) On the flipside, what would our financial world be like if Alan Greenspan had stayed a musician and not started keeping the books for the band in which he played? (He was the chairman of the Federal Reserve for a long time and managed our economy.) We all have something unique and wonderful about who we are. When we deny that, we steal from society and the world. There are hundreds of examples of people who have impacted the world, yet, were told to be something they were not.

You were put on this earth for a reason.

Chapter 10 – Bits of Hope

What about *you* is unique? When I was a middle and high school principal, I would take criticism for not focusing enough on the data of the content that was being produced in the classroom and that there were too many pep rallies allowed. My response was simple, everyone needs a reason to get out of bed in the morning. What is your reason? If you don't have one, what do you love to do? If you're not there yet, when was the last time you smiled, really smiled? What were you doing? What was that victory?

You were put on this earth for a reason.

Growing up overweight, I never thought I would be accused of being an adrenaline junkie. Five years earlier, I had stepped on a scale that read 302 pounds. The scale didn't lie; I had been overweight my whole life. It had been a few long years of dieting before I was able to have weight-loss surgery. I had gone from 302 down to 205. This was important because to complete this feat, one must be below 270 pounds. Now, I was standing on top of the largest building in Las Vegas connected to a cord and preparing to jump. This was a controlled descent off an 80-story tower; it was time to put up or shut up. The lady who was safety harnessed to the building next to me, and in charge of making sure I didn't die, yelled, "Ready 3, 2, 1, go." I stood there in fear. She looked at me as if to say, "You didn't go." I uttered "No, do it again." This time, I jumped. It takes approximately 13 seconds to fall 880 feet. The first three seconds you don't even realize that you're falling. I screamed all the way down, with a feeling of accomplishment at the end. My sister and niece were waiting at the bottom to congratulate me.

Chapter 10 – Bits of Hope

When I was in the process of preparation for surgery, I had people tell me not to do it, to stay the course or that things wouldn't be any better. For me, weight loss surgery was the right decision, however, that didn't stop people from trying to talk me out of it. "You don't need that surgery." "I'll bring you salads to eat at work." For me to make the change needed in my life, I had to be myself. Also, I was able to reap the reward that day. Those people who tried to talk me out of doing what was right for me didn't get to jump the building. This victory carries me through tough times.

Do the work

This is the hard side of the truth about being who you are. There is nothing in life that is accomplished without hard work. My parents went to college and finished raising their family at the same time. As a teenager, that meant having a front row seat watching a family tree change. I observed my mom getting up many days at five in the morning doing homework, going to class all day, and working until 10 at night. My dad did the same thing. He would get up, drive me to school and drive forty miles every day to run his business going from dog groomers, to barber shops, to hair salons, sharpening scissors and clipper blades all to pay the bills. At the same time, he would carry a full load of classes at the University. My parents drove a beat-up blue van with a sliding side door that was three shades of blue that didn't match. The driver's side doors were a cream color that also didn't match. Again, they didn't care because they were working hard to be successful.

There is no shortcut to success.

Chapter 10 – Bits of Hope

As a middle and high school principal, I tried to model myself after my parents. When I heard enough complaining from young people about their schedule, I would go into a "half-day in the life of a principal."

5:30 am Get up and get ready
6:30 am Go to a coffee place
6:45 am Four large coffee's
7:15 am Drive to work
7:30 am Drink one coffee, give away three
7:30 am-1:00 pm Do "principal-ly" stuff until one o'clock
1:00 pm-2:30 pm Lead a staff meeting
2:30 pm-3:30 pm Go to lunch with the coaching staff
3:30 pm-5:30 pm Spend two hours catching up on paperwork
5:30 pm-9:00 pm Attend Basketball games as the "Administrator on Duty"
9:00 pm-7:00 am Pull an all-nighter chaperoning the Senior lock-in
7:00 am-1:00 pm Be "Administrator on Duty" for the cheerleaders who are renting the school gym for a competition
1:15 pm Go home
1:30 pm Sleep

This is not fiction; it's a real day on the job, specifically on December 20, 2013. This did not include calling the police, helping a student who had self-inflicted cuts, talking to an angry parent, or calling the superintendent to update the school calendar.

There are no shortcuts to success.

Chapter 10 – Bits of Hope

At a time of career change, moving from being a traditional classroom educator and leader, to a speaker, trainer, and coach, I experienced a titanic level of fear. Having spoken in front of five hundred students on multiple occasions, I had the skills for public speaking down to a point. However, confidence to speak in front of adults was fleeting. There was a moment when I had to actually ask myself, "Are you gonna go for it or not?" Over a period of six weeks, I went to forty meet-ups, joined three Toastmaster's clubs, and introduced myself to random groups of strangers over and over again. In a short amount of time, I went from barely being able to communicate in front of others, to winning speech contests and eliminating groups of useless utterances from my speaking pattern.

Hard times will come, but they don't last
I've lost jobs, had a fiancé walk away, flunked out of school, missed car payments and have been to the bottom.

One must keep going.

In Las Vegas, there is a fascinating Museum. It's called the Neon Museum. The amazing thing is that this place is made up of signs that have all been thrown away. They got to the point that they were all burned-out and were deemed useless by the resort and hotel managers. They were all thrown away. Someone realized that what was being thrown away was art. A foundation was formed and the classic sign art was restored and saved from destruction. One piece, the former sign of the Treasure Island Resort is amazing. It is so large that it can be seen from space. Our lives function in the same way.

Chapter 10 – Bits of Hope

When we are at our lowest defeat, God is working to bring us victory. Like the signs in Las Vegas, our past defeats become our future art. Now, you can walk certain parts of the city and see these signs that were thrown away, restored to their former glory.

One must keep going.

Joshua chapter three tells of the crossing of the Jordan River. The people of Israel had served their penitence for their unbelief. They had spent their time in "work purgatory," wandering in the desert for forty years. Forty years of seeing the same sites, setting up tents, tearing them down and moving on. A new generation had grown up knowing small daily miracles that were taken for granted. This group had heard of the miracles of the exit from Egypt, but had not experienced it for themselves. This is akin to my generation's view of the Vietnam War. We grew up hearing about Vietnam. However, Nam wasn't something that affected us on a daily basis. Those of us born in the seventies heard about it but never understood what the big deal was, until September 11th. Then, our world changed immediately. Life was not simple and easy, but hard and complicated. Now there is a new generation that grew up in the shadow of September 11th, yet, they don't know life before, only after. This is where the Israelites were. They had heard of giant locusts, frogs everywhere, rivers turning to blood, and first-born sons dying. There was skepticism about crossing the Jordan because they had heard, but not seen. So much of our life is in that place, where we've heard, but not seen.

Chapter 10 – Bits of Hope

Eventually, after three days of waiting, the priests took up the Ark of the Covenant, carried it into the river, and the river dried up. The nation of Israel passed, and they entered from a season of defeat towards a season of victory. After Forty years in the desert, the people of Israel moved on to the next phase for their nation.

One must keep going.

My favorite verse growing up was Jeremiah 29:11 (NIV). "¹¹For I know the plans I have for you," declares the LORD, "plans to prosper you and not to harm you, plans to give you hope and a future." I was fascinated with the idea that God knew the outcomes in my life. I believed it and it is true. However, eventually people started pointing out to me, verses 12 and 13 "¹²Then you will call on me and come and pray to me, and I will listen to you. ¹³You will seek me and find me when you seek me with all your heart." This was a little disheartening, as I had focused only on the promise, and not the verses surrounding it. I had picked one verse in obscurity and didn't put it in any context. Verses 12 and 13 added a condition to God knowing his plans and the condition was that we needed to seek him. Seeking him is talking to him daily. I went to seminary and started looking for a job before I read verse 14. I believe the key to the chapter is verse 14. "I will be found by you," declares the LORD, "and will bring you back from captivity. I will gather you from all the nations and places where I have banished you," declares the LORD, "and will bring you back to the place from which I carried you into exile." (NIV) It's the shift. Verse 11 puts our future in God's hands.

Chapter 10 – Bits of Hope

Verse 12 and 13 put our future in our hands by adding the condition of seeking. Verse 14 brings them together. The key phrases are "I will be found by you" and "Where I have banished you." God claims responsibility for the banishment of the Israeli people. This is a hard one; a truth that must be accepted. Whatever we are going through, God has made it happen. He knows what will happen, and has promised to bring us out.

Final Thoughts

Don't let anyone tell you that you can't. We were fearfully and wonderfully made. The Bible says so in Psalms. Be You. You were put on this earth for a reason. Put in the work. There is no shortcut to success. Hard times come, but they don't last. One must keep going. These are the bits of hope. Keep them close to your heart, ready at your disposal for the future. You may run into a situation in life where you find yourself in "work purgatory." You may be stuck. The thought may run through your head, *"if I unbuckle my seatbelt….."* When this happens, look for your bits of hope. If you are sleeping in alleys and eating pork and beans, wining and dining with kings and queens is just around the corner.

- Nathan Riddle

Chapter 10 – Bits of Hope

About the Author – Nathan Riddle

Nathan Riddle has over twenty years of experience working with students, parents, and teachers as a former Dean of Instruction, teacher and secondary principal. He has worked with such stellar organizations as A+ Academies, Lifeway, Southwestern Baptist Theological Seminary, Zig Ziglar International, and Prestonwood Baptist Church. Whether leading a district-wide planning committee or working as a one-on-one coach, Nathan Riddle will always be a teacher.

Chapter 10 – Bits of Hope

Nathan's heart beats for helping future generations reach their dreams.

(469) 226-3901
Lifeguruorsomething.com
nathan@lifeguruorsomething.com
Facebook-Lifeguruorsomething

Chapter 10 – Bits of Hope

"When we are at our lowest defeat,
God is working to bring us victory."
Nathan Riddle

Chapter 11 – Dreams, Choices and Paths

Chapter 11

Dreams, Choices and Paths
By Ephraim Osunde - Nigeria

Two roads diverged in a wood, and I—
I took the one less traveled by,
And that has made all the difference.
- *From The Road Not Taken. By* <u>**Robert Frost**</u>

It was a Friday evening, and I was sitting in my room in the university hostel having just completed the final exams of my full-time MBA (Master of Business Administration) program. It was the culmination (climax) of a journey I embarked on almost two years earlier – a journey that I hoped would change my life trajectory, but I was unsure how it would play out. Looking back as I write 24 years later, it was indeed a life-changing, destiny-altering decision I took amidst difficult circumstances at the time.

However, as I sat alone in my room that Friday evening at the crossroads between the twilight of the MBA journey and the darkness of the uncertainties of the future, the only assurance I had that the dawn would really come was my

Chapter 11 – Dreams, Choices and Paths

unwavering belief in and commitment to my dream. This is my story of pursuing that dream which propelled me in the first place to undertake the MBA quest, the dream that saw me through the difficult terrain and deprivation I endured, the dream which opened up other horizons when the initial finishing line of pursuit had been crossed.

"Yes: I am a dreamer. For a dreamer is one who can only find his way by moonlight, and his punishment is that he sees the dawn before the rest of the world." - <u>Oscar Wilde</u>,

As I sat in that university room on that cool, breezy evening pondering over the future, I could not help, but cast my mind back to the genesis of this dream which I left my comfort zone to pursue.

It all began a few years after leaving the university and I started working at my first full-time employment. I began to have a feeling of restlessness, that feeling that says, "*I could be more than I am, I could be doing more and I could be accomplishing more.*" I kept asking, "*Is this all I was going to spend my life doing?*" I did not know the path to that "more," and the courage to further explore the dream was initially hindered by the fetters of my mindset and societal expectations. "What more do you want, young man," I seem to hear the restraining voice of my mind and society telling me. "You have a good job with excellent prospects, you should be grateful and there are many who will give a lot to trade places with you," added the voice. I even shared my discontent with my boss at the time,

Chapter 11 – Dreams, Choices and Paths

and I was promised that something more challenging and engaging will be found for me. But the restlessness grew.

I then knew I had to obey this other voice that challenged me to go out and explore the unknown, but seemingly exciting opportunities that beckoned. "After all," the voice said, "you are young and you have a professional qualification, so if you fail, you have something to fall back to." I did not see the full picture of the path to take at that time, but somehow, I knew the first step on that new path was to go back to school and get my MBA degree, which I strongly suspected would lead to other horizons. In retrospect, I have learned that in pursuing the dream(s) that God lays in our hearts, we may sometimes not know or see the full path, but if we believe in the dream, and the first steps are shown to us that is all we need to begin. The principle is "step upon step, line upon line, and a little here, a little there."

"Restlessness is discontent and discontent is the first necessity of progress. Show me a thoroughly satisfied man and I will show you a failure." – Thomas Edison

Part of my plan was to get another job closer to the university town where I planned to do the MBA and hopefully undertake it as a part-time program while holding my full-time job for financial reasons. The first part of the plan worked; I got another job similar to the one I had at the time the restlessness began. I got a tacit agreement from my supervisor to undertake the program part-time when the

Chapter 11 – Dreams, Choices and Paths

time came. However, soon after I got the admission, my other senior supervisors requested that I had to choose between the program and my job. This was an unforeseen dilemma I had to resolve.

My initial natural response was to contemplate deferring the admission as I was clearly unprepared for the financial burden of taking the program without the income flow from a substantive job. However, despite the effluxion of time, I still clearly recall the moment and place where (as I brooded over this situation and the decision I had to make), I perceived an unmistakably clear impression in the form of the following statement:
"What is the guarantee that if you defer the program to the following year, you will be granted the permission to take it with your job or that your financial circumstances will be better?"

Somehow, I knew right away that this was the guidance I was seeking from God on what to do.

I made the difficult, but ultimately rewarding decision (with hindsight) to leave the job and take the program that year. *"I will get a part-time job (with clearly lesser income than the one I was leaving), I will cut down my expenses and adjust my lifestyle in line with the reality I faced, and will complete the program,"* I reasoned to myself. I was under no illusion as to the required sacrifice, but having obtained the guidance I needed, I had no alternative but to commit myself to the required action. That was exactly what I did.

Chapter 11 – Dreams, Choices and Paths

Little did I know that this commitment would impact my life in more ways than I imagined and clearly beyond the dreams of getting my MBA.

"Unless commitment is made, there are only promises and hopes...but no plans." – Peter Drucker

"Clarity comes after commitment has been made."
– Ellie Drake

I have learned from this experience and many others that often times when we waver at the brink of pursuit of the dream planted in our hearts we give power to the spirit of double-mindedness to become a dream killer. I am not advocating that we should be impetuous in character and decision-making. We should clearly articulate and think carefully over our plans (arising from the dream in our hearts), we should do due diligence as much as we can and pray very well. Many times, we should seek counsel as input into the planning and decision making process. However, after all these, the time for commitment must come. No matter the amount of due diligence and prayers we make, there is always an element of risk in our decisions. We must be courageous and make the decision to move forward rather than be paralyzed and stuck in the slimy mud of indecision arising from fear.

Chapter 11 – Dreams, Choices and Paths

I made the decision to move forward (with a firm belief in my dream and God's guidance) and I got much more than the MBA and a career break in return.

As I found out much later, a young lady in another town far away from me was going through a similar situation. She was bored with her job, needed a break, and decided she would go for her MBA. Her admission letter came late and she was considering not continuing that year, but was persuaded by someone to follow through. It so happened we were joining the same class. We met during the program, became friends and two years after the course, we got married to each other.

As I write this chapter, we have been married for over 22 years and have four children - three lovely daughters and a son. Imagine if I had deferred the program for one year or if she did the same. We would have never met or had the privilege of sharing our lives over this long period of time and with an even greater future ahead.

Back to my reverie in my postgraduate university room that fateful Friday night, as I reflected on where I was coming from and what my direction was for the future. I could still not clearly articulate what exactly I was going to do with the MBA. Again, as I ruminated over the future, a burst of inspiration hit me. It seemed I heard the following words inside of me:

"Since you cannot identify the immediate path leading out from this present point, why don't you write down the characteristic of the next job you think will address your yearnings."

Chapter 11 – Dreams, Choices and Paths

Quickly, I reached for the notepad and pen beside my bed and began to paint a word picture of the next career path. Strangely, after this activity, I felt some light of clarity gradually emerging from the darkness of uncertainty. It happened just like the morning light of dawn always succeeds a night of impenetrable darkness. I was filled with a renewed sense of courage and hope to pursue what was no longer a phantom, as the outlined career characteristics bore close resemblance among others, to what was known then as brand or product management.

My main plan was clear: *since I had a degree in Pharmacy and an MBA, I would get into a junior management position as a product or brand manager (in a global/multinational pharmaceutical firm), and move on from there to a fulfilling career in marketing. Ultimately, I will rise to either the role of a marketing director or better still, a country general manager.* Of course, there were many other options I considered, for example, remaining in the quiet university town, getting a teaching job, and becoming a lecturer after further advanced degrees. Teaching and passing on knowledge was a nascent part of me which I imagined could find expression through this option. I chose the option of a career in the corporate world, and a few months after my graduation, moved to the commercial capital of my country to pursue this goal.

It became obvious that I would stand a better chance of getting the job if I was where the headquarters of most of the organizations were located. There was also a romantic perspective to the move as it provided an opportunity to be

Chapter 11 – Dreams, Choices and Paths

in the same town as my then wife-to-be, a step that facilitated the development of our relationship.

An interesting part of my odyssey emerged after I relocated to begin the search for the job. I was informed that a general criterion for getting such a job was sales experience. I had no prior sales experience in the industry. Some of my classmates who left pharmacy school seven years or so before then, and went straight into the industry as sales representatives, were already occupying similar or other managerial roles I was seeking. This was an obstacle I was determined to overcome. I was ready to go back seven years of my life (as it seemed at the time), to take a sales representative job, get the experience and move into the managerial role I desired.

I reckoned that with my maturity, cognate exposure, and the training I would receive, my progress would be rapid. I was, therefore, prepared to "stoop to conquer" and began to apply for sales representative positions. I had the unique and humbling experience of being interviewed on two occasions by my classmates (who had become managers because they entered the industry much earlier), but I bore it all with a measure of calmness and equanimity. On one of those sales representative interviews, I was even asked by the CEO, what relevance my MBA would have on my job as a sales representative. I was shocked to hear such a question, but I answered as best as I could.

Despite my inclination to take this different route to my goal, I did not get the sales representative job.

Chapter 11 – Dreams, Choices and Paths

I was told when I inquired about the reason, that they were not sure I would stay long. Given my mature circumstances, education and exposure, they were certain I would not spend more than a year or less before seeking a higher role elsewhere. This was certainly a correct analysis of my situation and, in a sense, I was glad I was not rejected for a perceived lack of confidence, but that paradoxically, I was overqualified.

As the months of search wore on, it became an increasingly discouraging period of my life. My financial situation was very poor, as I was barely surviving on a slim income from a part-time job in a local pharmacy outlet. This was hardly enough to pay for my transportation and feeding needs. I was tempted at some point to veer from my goal and search for a job completely at a variance with my avowed goal.

I received significant encouragement at those bleak moments from my then fiancée (who later became my wife). This helped me stay on course and gave me hope in believing that I would hit the mark. I also volunteered to undertake some work in my local church assembly when I was not working at my part-time job. This helped me shift my focus from my situation to helping others. A lesson learned here is that when we are going through our periods of difficulties in life, it helps to shift focus from ourselves, to how we could be of help to others. No matter how bad we think our situation may be, there is someone somewhere, we could be of help to.

Chapter 11 – Dreams, Choices and Paths

Sowing our time into the lives of others, has psychological and spiritual benefits apart from the unforeseen pecuniary rewards that may come sometimes.

About six months into my job search, a friend to my fiancée, working in one of the firms I was seeking to join, informed me about a couple of vacancies for product managers in her organization, to which I quickly applied. I was shortlisted for the interview which consisted of a test and a face-to-face interview. When I got into the hall for the test, there were quite a number of candidates, many with industry sales experience. I was not perturbed and went ahead to tackle the questions. I will never forget the exhilarating feeling I had when I was answering the main question in the test. In my opinion, it was a question that one could only effectively answer if one had gone through an MBA program or had considerable management experience. I felt satisfied I had done my best. To my joy, I was shortlisted for the final phase of the interview and I met with the managers of the company.

A few weeks later, I was offered the job as a product manager, despite not having any sales experience which many people had touted was a must for the job. I discovered that the other person offered the similar job of a product manager (there were two open positions), was a classmate of mine in pharmacy school who had also just obtained his MBA from another school at that time. Thus, my assumption regarding the relevance of MBA to success at the competency test was validated.

Chapter 11 – Dreams, Choices and Paths

In addition, my dream to pursue the MBA was vindicated to God's glory, and I felt equally glad that my sacrifices in pursuit of the dream were not in vain. I went on to have an interesting and fulfilling career with that organization. I garnered significant transferable skills that are still useful to me today. The experience with that organization opened up more horizons of that initial dream and led me into other paths that I could only have imagined.

I have always dreamt of doing work that I will be so glad to do for free because I enjoyed it, yet be blessed enough to be paid for it. I have met people who feel it is not possible. I have been there, and I am still there and no one can argue against my experience. The next part of the story of how I got there will be told another time. But now my work is my hobby and I get paid for doing it. I also learned the lesson epitomized by the famous and beautiful words of **Eleanor Roosevelt, *"The future belongs to those who believe in the beauty of their dreams."***

So dear friends, keep dreaming, keep believing, keep taking action and one day, your dream will become a reality.

I have had many other dreams since then and have worked to see the reality of many of them. I am still dreaming and will continue to do so, working at them, for without dreams, life is meaningless.

Chapter 11 – Dreams, Choices and Paths

God puts dreams in our hearts to pursue, for our benefits and ultimately, for His glory. Your dream could be the legacy that you leave on this earth when it becomes a reality.

May your path be blessed, may your dreams come through, and may you find success in what you do as you leave a positive mark on this planet.

- Ephraim Osunde

Chapter 11 – Dreams, Choices and Paths

About the Author – Ephraim Osunde

Ephraim Osunde is a seasoned organizational and learning development practitioner, consultant, internationally certified facilitator, speaker, and leadership coach. He draws from three decades of diverse post-graduation work experience within a variety of organizations (including seven exciting years of leading the independent consulting practice he founded). He is also a Ziglar Legacy Certified Trainer.

Although he originally trained and practiced as a licensed pharmacist, he holds three Master's Degrees in diverse, but integrated areas: MBA, Psychometrics (City University,

Chapter 11 – Dreams, Choices and Paths

London) and Business Technology Consulting (Henley, United Kingdom). All these have contributed to his present professional path. He is currently on the MPhil degree in Management Coaching at University of Stellenbosch Business School, Cape Town (South Africa), through which he hopes to develop a theoretical framework and authentic-contextual model for his coaching practice. He currently heads the Organizational Capability Division in a subsidiary of a Global Integrated Energy Company where he is responsible for setting and implementing strategies for workforce development, especially leadership development.

For the past 20 years, Ephraim has also served as a Pastor in a Pentecostal denomination. Apart from the pastoral leadership of his Local Assembly, he supervises many church pastors in his role as a Provincial Pastor.

He describes his mission as: *"To ignite and facilitate the discovery, development and deployment of potential in individuals and organizations towards achieving principle-centered significance."* He is married to his wife of twenty-two years and they are blessed with three daughters and a son.

eosunde2000@yahoo.com

+234-803-306-3998

Chapter 11 – Dreams, Choices and Paths

God puts dreams in our hearts to pursue, for our benefits and ultimately, for His glory. Your dream could be the legacy that you leave on this earth when it becomes a reality.

- Ephraim Osunde

EPILOGUE

Throughout my life, I have always felt a bigger and better purpose for my life, but I have not always been in pursuit of it, mostly because I have been my own biggest obstacle. I was often distracted by my current comfort zones through my current routines. They kept me from stepping into my full potential and kept me as a prisoner to my routines. I knew that I wanted to "walk with faith," I was just not focused enough to see it or empowered enough to make a change.

After years of very strong feelings that God had something better for me, I only took action to start changing my life, when I chose to have faith and act on God's plan for me. I knew this was the only way to fix my life.

Through His grace, I am a new man. I understand my purpose and I am full of life. I can see Him clearly, and I am stronger than ever.

With regard to success, I have always felt that my purpose was to help others through the gift of speaking. I have always dreamed of becoming a motivational/inspirational speaker, but for the largest part of my life, I only considered this a dream.
Who was I to be a speaker?
What credentials or gifts did I have?
These were negative thoughts that I burdened myself with.

So, who am I?
I am a son of our King.
I know Him and He knows me.

Today, all because of Him, and through my obedience to decide, take action and have faith, I am living my life's dream. I am pursuing my life's goal, and most importantly, my life's purpose to help others build their lives.

Believe in God and His plan for your life. Have faith and take action. You too can make all of your dreams come true because you are also the son or daughter of the same King!

Now Go Forth and Make YOUR Life Exceptional!

- **Mike Rodriguez**

About Mike Rodriguez

Mike Rodriguez is CEO of Mike Rodriguez International, a professional speaking, training and consulting firm. Besides being a Best-Selling author, he is a world-renowned motivator and a leadership and sales expert. Mike also owns a publishing company and still manages to spend quality time with his wife and their five daughters. He is a former showcase speaker with the world famous Zig Ziglar Corporation and was selected as their speaker and sales expert for the 2015 Ziglar U.S. Tour.

Mike delivers performance-based seminars and trainings and has authored several books which have been promoted by Barnes & Noble. He has been featured on CBS, U.S. News and World Report and has lectured at Baylor University, UNT and K-State Research. His clients include names like Hilton, McDonald's Corporation and the Federal Government. As a sales expert, Mike has trained thousands.

Everyone faces challenges; Mike believes that through faith and action, you can overcome the challenges in your life to attain your goals and become who you truly want to be.

Throughout his career, Mike has built productivity-driven training programs and managed multi-million dollar quotas. He has experience delivering powerful messages and creating personal development strategies for new and tenured companies and teams across many industries.

Mike has been happily married since 1991 to Bonnie, the love of his life. He believes if you have the right attitude and the right faith, you can have the right kind of success, regardless of the type of industry that you are in.

Walking with FAITH, Stories That Inspire

As a world-renowned speaker,
Mike has experience working with people
from all walks of life.

You can schedule Mike Rodriguez
to speak or train at your next event.
Go to:
www.MikeRodriguezInternational.com

Other books available by Mike Rodriguez:

Finding Your WHY

8 Keys to Exceptional Selling

Break Your Routines to Fix Your Life

M.A.P. Selling

Lion Leadership

Think BIG Motivational Quotes

Life Builders

Walking with FAITH, Stories That Inspire

Disclaimer & Copyright Information

Some of the events, locales, and conversations have been recreated from memories. In order to maintain their anonymity, in some instances, the names of individuals and places have been changed. As such, some identifying characteristics and details may have changed.

Although the authors and publishers have made every effort to ensure that the information in this book was correct at press time, the authors and publishers do not assume and hereby disclaim any liability to any party for any loss, damage, or disruption caused by errors or omissions, whether such errors or omissions result from negligence, accident, or any other cause.

All quotes, unless otherwise noted,
are attributed to the respective Authors or to the Holy Bible.

Cover illustration, book design and production
Copyright © 2016 by Mike Rodriguez International
www.TributePublishing.com

"Go Forth and Make Your Life Exceptional" ™
and "Go Forth and Sell Something!" ™
are copyrighted trademarks of the Author, Mike Rodriguez.

Scripture references are copyrighted by www.BibleGateway.com
which is operated by the Zondervan Corporation, L.L.C

"I can do ALL THINGS through Christ who strengthens me."
Philippians 4:13

NOTES

NOTES

NOTES

www.ingramcontent.com/pod-product-compliance
Lightning Source LLC
Chambersburg PA
CBHW021126300426
44113CB00006B/312